The Seven Standards

Of Ecological Breastfeeding

The Frequency Factor

Sheila K. Kippley

THE SEVEN STANDARDS OF ECOLOGICAL
BREASTFEEDING: THE FREQUENCY FACTOR, first edition.
Copyright © 2008 by Sheila Kippley

All rights reserved. No part of this book may be reproduced in any
manner whatsoever without written permission of the copyright holder
except in the case of brief quotations in articles and reviews.

Other books by Sheila Kippley:
    Breastfeeding and Natural Child Spacing, 1969, 1974, 1975,
        1989, 1999, 2008
    Breastfeeding and Catholic Motherhood, 2005
    The Art of Natural Family Planning (with John Kippley) 1972,
        1979, 1984, 1996.
    Natural Family Planning (with John Kippley), 2005

This book explains how mothers can breastfeed their babies in a way
that normally postpones the return of postpartum fertility. This is a
natural side effect. While this book refers to health and nutritional
benefits of breastfeeding, it is not intended to provide professional
health, medical or nutritional advice. Individuals with a personal health
problem or whose children have health problems should seek the help
of competent health-care professionals.

ISBN: 978-1-4357-4622-0

Contents

Foreword by Teresa Pitman   v

Introduction   vii

Chapter One and First Standard
    Breastfeed Exclusively for the First Six Months   1
Chapter Two and Second Standard
    Pacify Your Baby at Your Breasts   9
Chapter Three and Third Standard
    Don't Use Bottles and Pacifiers   15
Chapter Four and Fourth Standard
    Sleep with Your Baby for Night Feedings   21
Chapter Five and Fifth Standard
    Sleep with Your Baby for a Daily-Nap Feeding   37
Chapter Six and Sixth Standard
    Nurse Frequently Day and Night
    and Avoid Schedules   45
Chapter Seven and Seventh Standard
    Avoid Any Practice That Restricts Nursing
    or Separates You from Your Baby   53
Chapter Eight
    Natural Weaning and the Return of Fertility   69
Chapter Nine
    Natural Child Spacing   83
Chapter Ten
    Systematic NFP and Support   95

The Seven Standards Summary   103

Breastfeeding Survey   105

Foreword

When I had my first baby, at my postpartum visit the doctor asked me about my plans for birth control. I said that since I was exclusively breastfeeding, I wasn't concerned. He told me that breastfeeding was completely unreliable when it came to preventing pregnancy, and that I'd be back in a few weeks crying because I was pregnant again. His condescending attitude offended me as much as his misinformation!

Fortunately, I knew it was misinformation because my La Leche League Leader had shown me a copy of *Breastfeeding and Natural Child Spacing*. That wonderful, warm book not only helped me understand how breastfeeding helped to regulate my fertility, it helped me to better understand how my body worked and to recognize the meaning of the changes I saw.

I'm glad to say that we have made some progress in the decades since my son's birth. I rarely hear mothers being told that breastfeeding doesn't affect fertility. But women often don't know that *how* they breastfeed and care for their babies can make all the difference in terms of effectiveness.

This new book provides the solution. The essential information is all here, clearly explained and enhanced by current research and personal stories from mothers who have used these concepts in their own lives. With these guidelines to help, mothers can enjoy an extended period of natural infertility. But there are other benefits, too. These guidelines encourage you to stay close to your baby and respond to his or her needs – creating an attachment between the two of you that becomes the foundation of the mother-child relationship.

In fact, one of the things I have always liked best about the way breastfeeding spaces babies is that it is responsive to the needs of the individual baby. If you have a high-need baby, who nurses frequently around the clock well into toddlerhood, you'll probably find your fertility takes longer to return. That means this child has more time to receive the focused attention he or she needs.

There are many books on breastfeeding, and many that mention the value of breastfeeding in delaying the return of menstruation (which has many benefits for mothers besides that of preventing another pregnancy too soon). But this book is unique. This is the only book that answers all the questions mothers might ask about how breastfeeding affects their reproductive cycles, and how they can fit an ecological approach to breastfeeding into their busy families.

Teresa Pitman
Executive Director of La Leche League Canada 2003-2007
Co-author of *The Ultimate Breastfeeding Book of Answers*
   (with Dr. Jack Newman),
The Latch and Other Keys to Successful Breastfeeding
   (with Dr. Jack Newman),
Pregnancy and Birth: Making the Decisions that are Right for You and Your Baby
(with Dr. Joyce Barrett) and nine other books on parenting topics

Introduction

The purpose of this book is to provide experience-based support to health-care providers for the practice of the Seven Standards of ecological breastfeeding. I use "health-care providers" in the wide sense of parents, physicians, nurses, lactation consultants, social workers, and pastors and other church workers who offer support to mothers and infants.

Clarity requires distinctions, and so this book will distinguish between those forms of nursing that have almost no effect upon postpartum fertility and the form of breastfeeding that does have a significant effect.

Clarity also requires a definition: Ecology is concerned with the relationships between two organisms and how each affects the other. *Ecological breastfeeding is the form of nursing in which the mother fulfills her baby's needs for frequent suckling and her full-time presence and in which the child's frequent suckling postpones the return of the mother's fertility.* Both parties, mother and baby, benefit from this relationship.

The basis of this book is experience. Some of this experience comes from scientific studies. Some of it comes from the widespread anecdotal experience of breastfeeding mothers. Frequent nursing is the basic requirement for maintaining both an ample supply of milk and the normal suppression of fertility. While that is the reality, most mothers seem to be unaware of it unless they are properly instructed. The Seven Standards provide the rules or the proper instruction for the frequent and unrestricted nursing associated with ecological breastfeeding.

About some things there should be no debate. There are so many health benefits of breastfeeding that every health-care provider and supporter ought to be doing what they can to promote it. These benefits increase with duration. Frequency of nursing is necessary to stimulate the regular production of milk. Only the frequent nursing of ecological breastfeeding or something very close to it provides the sort of continuous milk supply enjoyed by mothers and their babies in less-developed cultures that are more in tune with nature.

Further, there should be no debate that ecological breastfeeding IS a form of natural child spacing. To be sure, it seems that almost everyone has heard of breastfeeding mothers who became pregnant only three or four months postpartum, but that simply highlights the difference between cultural breastfeeding and ecological breastfeeding. Cultural breastfeeding has almost no effect on postpartum fertility. I acknowledge that even with ecological breastfeeding, there can be an occasional very early return of fertility, but the demonstrated reality is that the early return is very far from the average and it cannot be regarded as the norm. Every health-care provider should know the differences between cultural and ecological breastfeeding, and they should do what they can to encourage the latter.

This is my third book on breastfeeding. In my first book, *Breastfeeding and Natural Child Spacing: The Ecology of Natural Mothering*, I emphasized the mothering aspects of ecological breastfeeding for spacing babies and focused on the personal mother-baby ecology. First published in 1969, it was revised and republished by Harper & Row in 1974. After several editions over the years, the "classic" Harper & Row edition, with only a few updates, is being republished this year.

My second book, *Breastfeeding and Catholic Motherhood*, published in 2005 by Sophia Institute Press, was occasioned by the realization that countless numbers of Catholic mothers seemed to be completely unaware that the Catholic Church encourages mothers to breastfeed if at all possible. Further, at a time when many of them talk about the "theology of the body" developed by the late Pope John Paul II, they seem to be unaware that this applies to breastfeeding. Thus, *Breastfeeding and Catholic Motherhood* focuses on the spiritual and contemporary theological reasons for breastfeeding in general and especially for ecological breastfeeding.

This work, *The Seven Standards*, focuses on the maternal behaviors that are involved with ecological breastfeeding. It makes easily available the research the supports these practices.

Some might wonder why the 1974 edition of *Breastfeeding and Natural Child Spacing* and *The Seven Standards of Ecological Breastfeeding* are being published at the same time. The first book's focus is more on mothering while the latter book's focus is more on the specific behaviors of the Seven Standards. The research, stories, and quotes are different in each book. I was also swayed by a dear friend who promotes ecological breastfeeding. In her opinion, the classic *Breastfeeding and Natural Child Spacing* was her favorite book on this topic.

> Of all the editions, I still love the Harper & Row edition. I started reading it again, and it drew me in all over again. I could hardly put it down. I still love it so much. I believe *The Seven Standards* needs to be written for the more scholarly, research-based information. There was such an emphasis in the classic edition on how countercultural eco-breastfeeding was and how very much the culture is against it and leads against it. It was a bit like an expose of how the culture is trying to take away my authentic womanhood by replacing me with mother-substitutes. Also in the classic, the notion of the ecological relationship was woven in and seemed to come up again and again, not so much explicitly but subtly. Now that I am reading the classic, I just love it all over.

The two books are significantly different. I hope interested readers enjoy both of them.

With regard to *The Seven Standards*, each Standard is important. Thus I devote a chapter to each of the Seven Standards. Since I speak often of mother and baby, I have chosen to give the baby masculine pronouns for clarity and at times have chosen to address the mother personally. The short quotations at the beginning and end of each chapter are from mothers who corresponded with me over the years. I hope this book is helpful to many.

--*Sheila Kippley*
July 2008

1

First Standard

Breastfeed Exclusively for the First Six Months

"My second child is now 7½ months old. I haven't had a period yet. I breastfed him exclusively until 6½ months when he wanted food from my plate. I learned from experience that I must be careful about solids. My baby nurses twice at night and for long periods of time."

Exclusive breastfeeding takes place when you give your baby nothing but your milk; that is, the baby's only nutrition and hydration is milk suckled directly from your breasts. A normal healthy baby does not need water, other liquids or solids during the first six months of life. The healthiest gift you can give your baby is to exclusively breastfeed him for the first six months of life. Breast milk is sufficient for nutrition and hydration.

What's the first step for breastfeeding infertility?
Exclusive breastfeeding is an important first step to take if you want the side benefit of breastfeeding infertility. The truth is when you provide 1) all of your baby's nourishment at your breasts and 2) the greater part of his other sucking needs at your breasts, you will almost invariably experience the side effect of natural infertility. To have that side effect for more than a few weeks or months, however, requires something more. Exclusive breastfeeding is an important part of ecological breastfeeding, but it is not the whole picture.

Exclusive breastfeeding without the rest of the Seven Standards of eco-breastfeeding may mean an early return of menstruation.

With exclusive breastfeeding the baby is receiving all of his nourishment from his mother's breasts, but the nursing may not be frequent enough to hold back menstruation. Research shows that almost half of the exclusively breastfeeding mothers using the above rule alone will experience menstruation prior to six months.[1] This is why mothers who are interested in natural child spacing are often taught to nurse more frequently, to nurse during the night, to avoid letting too many hours lapse between feedings, and to avoid pacifiers. When mothers nurse more frequently day and night, exclusive breastfeeding is more likely to suppress menstruation and ovulation during the first six months postpartum.

Why isn't exclusive breastfeeding sufficient for natural infertility?

The exclusive breastfeeding rule says nothing about frequency. Some mothers have been very disappointed to experience menstruation or conception while following the "exclusive breastfeeding" rule for postpartum infertility. Quite often these mothers are not nursing frequently enough to maintain natural infertility. We have learned that exclusive breastfeeding by itself is no guarantee that menstruation or ovulation will not occur. A mother who exclusively breastfeeds primarily for *nutrition* may not be satisfying her child's other needs for comfort and bonding at the breast.

Babies need frequent suckling.

Taking nature as the norm, frequent nursing is normal for a baby. There is no reason to discourage the needs of the baby which are met easily and naturally at the breast. It is usually easier for the mother to nurse her baby for a few minutes than to spend time trying to satisfy her baby by other means. It is easier on the ears as well. Who wants to listen to a crying baby?

One of your baby's strongest instinctive behaviors is sucking. Sucking is his primary means to obtain nourishment and comfort from you, his mother. Just as you provided your baby's total nourishment in the womb, with exclusive breastfeeding you are now providing his total nourishment at your breasts. His frequent suckling at your breasts day and night is important because it stimulates a steady production of milk. The more he nurses, the more milk you will produce for him. The less he nurses, the less milk you will produce. It's a classic case of demand and supply. If you do not feel you have enough milk, you can nurse him more frequently during the day. You can also try to get more rest, especially by taking a long nap if possible during the day and letting your baby nurse during the nap. The extra nursings plus the added rest or nap normally increase the production of milk.

Exclusive breastfeeding for six full months is important for natural infertility.

Research since the mid-1950s has consistently shown that the introduction of solids and other liquids during the early months after childbirth is associated with an early return of fertility. Giving early foods or liquids to a baby under six months of age usually lessens the amount of nursing that takes place at the breast. Such supplements interfere with the frequent, unrestricted, and exclusive nursing needed to maintain natural infertility.

Exclusive breastfeeding is 98-99% effective in postponing pregnancy when three conditions are present:

1. The baby is not yet six months old
2. The mother has had no menstrual bleeding after the 56th day postpartum.
3. The breastfeeding is truly "exclusive" breastfeeding.[2]

Once your baby is six months old, or once you experience any menstrual bleeding after the first 8 weeks postpartum (56 days), or once you are no longer exclusively breastfeeding, the effectiveness of this rule no longer applies. This rule is called the Lactational Amenorrhea Method and has been heavily researched. La Leche League International (LLLI) began teaching a similar "exclusive breastfeeding" rule as far back as the Sixties.

In addition, research supports the conclusion that any vaginal bleeding in the first 56 days after childbirth can be ignored **if the mother is exclusively breastfeeding.**[3] Thus a mother who is doing exclusive breastfeeding *during* the first 56 days after childbirth will know that she is naturally infertile even if she experiences vaginal bleeding during that time. If she continues to exclusively breastfeed and has no bleeding *after* the 56th day, she is 98-99% infertile until her baby turns six months of age or until she has menstrual bleeding or until she stops exclusive breastfeeding—whichever comes first.

The exclusive breastfeeding rule is effective, is easy to teach, and is helpful to many nursing mothers, even for working mothers who want to nurse during their maternity leave.

Exclusive breastfeeding offers emotional nurturing for both mother and baby.

The emotional benefits of breastfeeding should be valued as much as the physical benefits of breastfeeding. More and more emphasis today is being placed on the importance of skin-to-skin contact between parent and child. Physical contact generates warm feelings of being loved and appreciated. Exclusive breastfeeding guarantees that the child will receive frequent physical contact from his mother during those first six months of life.

What happens to a mother during those first six months? First, she is discovering that breastfeeding is generally a very satisfying and enjoyable experience for her. She is also learning how to be a good mother in an easy environment. Through breastfeeding she learns to sacrifice her desires and time for the benefit of her baby. There may be some difficult times when she has to nurse and comfort her baby for long periods of time and the nursing is inconvenient. Yet she accepts this inconvenience because in her heart she knows that it is the right thing to do.

The importance of exclusive breastfeeding is that this emotional nurturing and intimate physical contact between mother and baby gets both off to an excellent start.

How long should a mother exclusively breastfeed?

Today almost every medical and breastfeeding organization at the national and world levels is asking mothers to nurse exclusively for the first six months of life. Breastfeeding research shows overwhelmingly the health advantages for both mother and baby. The more the mother breastfeeds and the longer she breastfeeds, the better the infant and maternal health outcomes. UNICEF states, "If all babies were fed only breastmilk for the first six months of life, the lives of an estimated 1.5 million babies would be saved every year and the health and development of millions of others would be greatly improved."[4]

If a mother can exclusively breastfeed for one month, that is better than not doing it at all. If a mother can do it for two months, that is even better. Will a baby benefit from 4 months of exclusive breastfeeding? Most likely. Babies exclusively breast-fed for four months have 56% fewer hospital admissions during the first year of life.[5]

Would it be better for a baby if a mother exclusively breastfeeds for six months instead of four months? Do two months make that much of a difference? Yes, they do. Babies breastfed exclusively for four months, but less than six months, had double the risk of recurrent middle ear infections and four times the risk of pneumonia between the ages of 6 and 24 months compared to those babies breastfed exclusively for six months.[6]

More studies are showing the benefits of exclusive breastfeeding. Canadian researchers who studied almost 14,000 children up to the age of 6½ years of age found strong evidence that prolonged and exclusive breastfeeding improves children's cognitive development.[7]

The World Cancer Research Fund stressed the importance of education to the general public about the importance of preventing cancer through breastfeeding. Why? Because "there is convincing scientific evidence that it protects against breast cancer" and that breastfeeding "probably protects the child against being overweight and obese, which is important for cancer prevention because being overweight increases cancer risk." What is the World Cancer Research Fund's recommendation to prevent cancer? "We recommend that if they are able to, mothers aim to breastfeed exclusively for the first six months and then continue with complementary feeding after that."[8]

For a healthier baby and a healthier mother, this simple guideline of exclusive breastfeeding is one most mothers can follow. All mothers should be encouraged to **exclusively**

breastfeed their baby for the first six months of life if at all possible.

Too many mothers quit nursing soon after childbirth or soon are no longer exclusively breastfeeding. These mothers need encouragement to persevere in exclusively breastfeeding their baby. Both mother and baby will be healthier as a result. In addition, these mothers will probably have a successful breastfeeding experience. They will also be following one of the Seven Standards for extended breastfeeding infertility. This natural plan benefits everyone in so many ways.

> This was the first baby exclusively breastfed for six months, and also a true baby-led weaning. The baby nursed very infrequently, but gained three pounds every month for the first six months except one month he gained four pounds. I am currently nursing our 17 month old without a return of my periods.

* * *

> Our son is a gift from God. Some of the happiest times with him have been nursing him following the ecological breastfeeding guidelines. He was 18 pounds by his four-month checkup, though at birth he was only six pounds. My husband and I are very thin and everyone jokes that he's not ours. They are even more surprised when we say he just nurses. It's been so easy and enjoyable to nurse him at night in our bed. He's a very contented baby and has brought us a lot of happiness.

* * *

> I think 100% breastfeeding is the only way to start a baby out in this complex world of ours. For me, it was the most wonderful experience of motherhood I have ever had.

1. Pérez, A., Labbok, M., and Queenan, J. "Clinical study of the lactational amenorrhoea method for family planning," *The Lancet*, Vol. 339, April 18, 1992.

2. "Consensus Statement: Breastfeeding as a Family Planning Method," *The Lancet*, November 19, 1988.
3. Ibid.
4. UNICEF. "Facts for Life," 2002.
5. Murata, P. and Barclary, L., "Full Breast-feeding May Lower Hospitalizations for Infections during First Year of Life," online at www.medscape.com/viewarticle/540857, *Pediatrics*, July 2006.
6. Chantry, C. et al., "Full Breastfeeding Duration and Associated Decrease in Respiratory Tract Infection in US Children," *Pediatrics*, 117 (February 2006) 425-432.
7. Kramer, M. et al., "Breastfeeding and Child Cognitive Development," *Archives of General Psychiatry*, 65:5 (2008) 578-584.
8. World Cancer Research Fund press release, "Most women unaware breastfeeding can prevent cancer," April 28, 2008. Available at www.wcrf-uk.org.

2

Second Standard

Pacify Your Baby at Your Breasts

"My baby sucked her fingers a lot the first three months when I tried halfheartedly to follow a schedule. She stopped when I relaxed and nursed her as often and as long as she needed."

Pacification at the breast is important for breastfeeding infertility. The extra non-nutritive or comfort suckling at the breast is nature's way of providing those extra hormonal surges in the woman's body that help to maintain natural infertility. Pacification at the breast is nature's way of comforting the baby and is an essential practice for natural child spacing. Regular use of the pacifier interferes with this natural plan.

Pacifier use has been "associated with an earlier return of menstruation."[1] Since pacifiers are known to reduce the amount of suckling at the breast, pacifiers should not be used on a regular basis by those mothers interested in natural child spacing.

Babies enjoy being pacified at the breast.
Babies have a natural need to suck for non-nutritive reasons. It's a need best satisfied at the mother's breasts. This habit is so natural that babies are known to comfort themselves by sucking their thumb or fingers in the womb. This natural suckling at the breast comforts most babies when they are tired, upset, hurt or scared. Comfort nursing should be widely promoted. Our society spends a great deal of time writing books on how to put babies to sleep. However, the easiest way to put a baby to sleep is to let the

baby nurse at his mother's breast. The same applies if the baby is fussy. Artificial pacifiers are used to calm and quiet a baby. The same results are usually accomplished with breastfeeding.

There are benefits for the breastfed baby who is not given a pacifier. Here are some of these benefits:
    1. likely reduction or avoidance of thumb-sucking or finger-sucking
    2. better and earlier speech
    3. better dental and facial development
    4. emotional satisfaction from increased contact with his mother
    5. more frequent nursing during the day and night
    6. longer duration of breastfeeding

There are reasons for not using a pacifier if you want to nurse successfully. The regular use of pacifiers tends to have the following effects:
    1. Pacifiers tend to shorten the suckling time at the breast.
    2. Pacifiers tend to reduce the number of breastfeeding sessions a mother has with her baby during the day.
    3. Pacifiers tend to shorten the duration of breastfeeding (the number of months that the mother nurses).
    4. Pacifiers have been shown to shorten the duration of exclusive breastfeeding.
    5. Heavy pacifier use may cause breastfeeding problems.

    We used pacifiers with our first baby. We found them to be a nuisance. I say "pacifiers" because most parents have more than one pacifier around the home. We did not use pacifiers with our last four children and did not miss them.

The breast brings love and closeness.
    The most important need for the baby is to be loved. To be close to mother on a regular basis, in her arms, at her breast, by her side, on her body is all the baby wants. Nature provides the baby with this closeness to the mother when he suckles at the breast for a variety of reasons. When the baby is tired, he seeks the breast. When the baby is in a new situation or is hurt, he seeks

comfort at the breast. In other words, breastfeeding provides much more than nutrition. Through breastfeeding the mother provides a lesson in love and trust for her baby. These breastfeeding moments are building blocks in giving any baby a healthy emotional and loving foundation for life.

Does breastfeeding mean that you as a mother have to give 100% of your attention to your baby? No. There are many times when you will be doing other activities or conversing with others and your attention will be diverted. But in whatever situation a busy mother finds herself, the physical closeness and love she has for her baby is still present and continues to be present through her breastfeeding—even if she is involved with company or another activity. Breastfeeding has an expansive influence upon both mother and baby. It is a simple, ordinary, and constant event that yields many benefits.

Non-nutritive suckling at the breast is important.

A mother might not use the pacifier, but she also might not allow for the non-nutritive suckling at the breast that the baby needs. For natural child spacing, a mother should allow for the non-nutritive sucking needs of her baby.

The *rare* use of a pacifier would probably not interfere with the natural infertility of breastfeeding for most women. A common example of a one-time use would be when a sibling wants to put the pacifier in the crying baby's mouth when traveling in the car for a short time because the mother is unable to stop the car to take care of her baby.

When the nutritional and emotional sucking needs of the infant are satisfied at the breast, they reinforce the mother-baby ecology and tend to postpone the return of fertility and menstruation. To take care of these needs, the mother remains physically close to her baby so she can respond easily day and night to the various needs of her infant.

Does the mother need to teach her baby how to pacify himself at the breast?

Some babies suck their thumb or fingers in the womb. If this is the case, your baby might have the habit of sucking his thumb or finger outside the womb. You can watch for this habit after birth. If your baby begins to suck on a finger or thumb, you can hold the involved hand and teach your baby to nurse instead. You can hum or sing to the baby when he uses the breast instead of his fingers or thumb. In other words, you can try to teach him in a loving way that the breast can satisfy this sucking urge of his as well as provide him with nutrition.

A pacifier does not have to be in the home.

Most people will assume that your baby will need a pacifier. I encourage you to be different. You do not need to have a pacifier in your home. You will find that nursing a baby to sleep or for comfort is a very satisfying experience. It is also a quiet event and something you can do while talking with friends, family or husband. One evening my husband and I were in our living room conversing with a friend. It finally dawned on her that I had nursed our toddler to sleep while we were talking and that I did it without any effort on my part. She couldn't believe it. Yet this is a wonderful advantage in favor of breastfeeding, the ease of putting a baby to sleep.

Pacifiers strongly influence mothering today. They are of special interest here since they limit the amount of nursing and mothering at the breast. Pacifiers replace the mother's natural role which is to calm and quiet her baby at the breast.

Breastfeeding provides the comfort.

No matter how young or how old your baby is, breastfeeding is an excellent way to pacify a little one. It's important to use the breast for all these reasons, and not just for food. In addition, if you are interested in natural child spacing, you will seriously consider using your breasts, instead of pacifiers, to meet the non-nutritive suckling needs of your baby. It is important to remember that mothering practices—such as using or not using a pacifier—can significantly influence the length of breastfeeding infertility.

> We have raised our baby the *hard way*—no baby swings and no pacifiers, and seldom am I out of her sight. Everyone tells me how carefree and easy those baby swings are and say that I am making life harder without one. I don't tell them it frightens

me to see their baby with a trancelike stare on its face—back and forth, back and forth for an hour! Yikes.

* * *

I love your coverage of real, natural mothering. People tell me I hold my baby too much, feed her too often, should give her a pacifier, and should not sleep with her. I ignore it all. How can my family possibly be happier?

* * *

I now believe that I overused a pacifier with my first baby and subsequently ran down my milk supply. I could never regain my confidence and my milk supply. I was very depressed that I ruined something so important to me. I now have a boy who is 11 months old and we enjoy a successful nursing relationship.

* * *

My third child had always been a difficult nurser. I nursed him anytime he wanted. At 16 months we rid him of his pacifier and nursing became a joy. From personal experience of nursing both culturally and ecologically, the difference is night and day for both baby and me. Ecological breastfeeding definitely made me feel closer to my baby.

1. Ingram J; Hunt L; Woolridge M; Greenwood R: "The association of progesterone, infant formula use and pacifier use with the return of menstruation in breastfeeding women," *European. Journal of Obstetrics &. Gynecology and. Reproductive Biology*, 114 (June 2004) 197-202.

3

Third Standard

Don't Use Bottles and Pacifiers

"I have never given my baby a bottle and don't plan to. Since reading your book, I've taken her off rice cereal and baby food which made her constipated anyway. My husband and I plan to take her with us to Key West, Florida on a trip my husband earned through his job. I am so thankful that he supports me in the breastfeeding and understands why I can't leave her home during that trip, even with the most trusted caregivers."

Avoid the use of bottles and pacifiers. This rule is implied with the First Standard of exclusive breastfeeding and the Second Standard of pacification at the breast. However, today there are a few mothers who exclusively breastfeed their baby by means of bottles and never put their baby to breast. This happens occasionally when a mother has difficulty breastfeeding and she pumps her milk and gives it to her baby via a bottle. Others may want to come and go as they please, so they say, never breastfeeding but pumping and feeding nothing but their bottled milk. For the record, such a baby-care regimen is not ecological breastfeeding.

One of the most common remarks made to nursing mothers is the negative question, "You don't want to be a pacifier to your baby, do you?" This question implies that your baby will always be at the breast, especially today when it is so common to see a baby with a pacifier in his mouth. The inference is that if the baby frequently has a pacifier in his mouth, then certainly he will likewise want the breast frequently in his mouth. Fortunately, that is not the case. This question also implies that the mother does not want to comfort her baby. Almost every mother wants to comfort her baby and this happens naturally with breastfeeding.

Cup feeding of breast milk is also not recommended if your baby is under six months of age. In fact, solids are offered at about six to eight months of age when a baby is exclusively breastfed. You can continue to offer breast milk at the breast for the baby's only liquid diet for several months after the baby begins solid food.

Nature's way is best.

Bottles and pacifiers are not necessary in normal situations when mother is present, but yet they are commonly used today. There are usually two assumptions when a mother is near her due date: she must buy several pacifiers and bottles for her baby and she must buy a pump for herself. These two assumptions are false unless the mother has to return to work and leave her baby.

Remember that you and your husband can do a good job of parenting without these two items. My husband and I discovered it was more rewarding to parent without them.

Baby carriers or slings can replace the pacifier.

A baby is usually quite happy and comfortable when he is with his mother. That is why in many cultures mothers have found a variety of ways to keep the baby on her person. Today there are many cloth carriers that keep the baby on the mother's person as she takes walks, makes a meal, or shops. I used a variety of baby carriers. I made a sling out of 2½ yards of sturdy 36" fabric. I double knotted the cloth sling for security and placed the bulky knot on my back. The fabric tucked under his bottom and supported his head. If it was windy or sunny, the extra fabric could cover his head for protection. I found carriers helpful for a variety of activities and walks. You can find a variety of baby carriers at breastfeeding conferences, local breastfeeding meetings, and online at various breastfeeding websites.

In addition, a poncho or shawl made of various fabrics (depending upon the weather) can also offer support to the baby when carried in front of his mother. The one side of the fabric in front can be wrapped around the baby; thus the baby is supported by the fabric and mother's arm, and the mother's other arm is free. A poncho also provides modesty when nursing in public because the fabric can be brought up higher around the mother's shoulders at this time.

Working mothers

Natural child spacing via breastfeeding is usually not a goal for mothers who work and leave their babies for eight or nine hours a day, five days a week. But some working mothers may find that they can remain in amenorrhea by nursing their baby during the night and whenever they can be available to their baby. Working mothers should avoid pumping their milk as quickly as possible and should pump only one breast at a time if they are interested in the possibility of natural spacing. More frequent pumping at a slower rate is recommended so that the pumping best resembles a nursing baby at the breast.

As the millennium started, a study found that working mothers who followed the exclusive breastfeeding rule for family planning had a cumulative pregnancy rate of 5.2% during the first six months; half of the working mothers in this study exclusively breastfed for the full six months postpartum, and half of those working mothers remained in amenorrhea at six months postpartum.[1] This 5.2% chance of pregnancy for those working mothers practicing the exclusive breastfeeding rule during the first six months after childbirth is similar to the 6% pregnancy rate of breastfeeding mothers who rely on amenorrhea and conceive before having had a menstrual period *regardless of the type of breastfeeding* and the length of amenorrhea.[2,3]

In another study, working mothers who took their breastfeeding seriously had different amenorrhea rates related to place of employment. Mothers who worked away from home, whether part-time or full-time, averaged 8.2 months of amenorrhea, while mothers who worked at home averaged 13.9 months of amenorrhea.[4]

Breastfeeding success may not come easily.

I encourage mothers who have problems with breastfeeding to keep trying. One acquaintance with a Down's syndrome baby offered the breast repeatedly but did not want to force the issue as her baby showed no interest. Finally, about four months later the baby started nursing on the breast and began to use only her breast for food and pacification. She was taken by surprise. Obstacles to breastfeeding can be overcome with love and patience. Sometimes a mother does not succeed with breast-feeding. She should feel good that she at least gave it her best try. All mothers need support—whether they succeed at breastfeeding or not. ***We must remember that it is the mother who is the most important person to the baby in this whole process, not just her milk.***

Bottles and pacifiers interfere with natural infertility.

The Third Standard, "Don't use bottles and pacifiers," is a very important rule to follow. It has to be included for emphasis in our bottle-feeding society. When a mother remains with her baby, these items are not needed. By following the Third Standard, you are more likely to experience an extended period of natural infertility.

> Your book has helped me by validating my efforts and is priceless for the encouragement it offers, especially in dealing with unsolicited advice from people who tell us, 'You're spoiling the baby!' I wonder how the human race has survived when a two-week-old baby is considered spoiled if picked up when he cries. We would be a healthier race if all mothers responded to their babies' cries and if schedules, pacifiers, and cribs were never invented.

* * *

> Our baby would not take a pacifier or any bottle. She would only nurse. Therefore, she went everywhere with us. This was fine with my husband and me, and our baby was happy and content.

* * *

> In looking back, I would embrace the practice of natural mothering all over again for each baby. I fondly reflect on all the times I gazed down at my nursing child with awe and great

love. What a perfect arrangement for mother and baby to bond and nurture one another. At times I reflect on what it would have been like to have bottle-fed my babies and left them with sitters frequently. I'm sure our life would have been different, but certainly not better. I thank God for showing me his mothering plan and natural family planning from the start of our marriage.

* * *

I have five breastfed children, but it wasn't always easy. With the first one I felt tied down with breastfeeding. I made sure she would take a bottle so I could get out and get away once in a while. When I look back now, the problem was that I wasn't comfortable nursing around others. I have overcome this. I have taken my nursing babies to concerts and picnics—even to the Democratic County Convention. Going on nature hikes is easy with a nursing baby. I've nursed the baby at church by covering the baby with a blanket. It's also nice to nurse the baby and read to a preschooler at the same time. The truth has set me free.

1. Valdés, V. et al. "The efficacy of the Lactational Amenorrhea Method among working women," *Contraception*, 62 (2000) 217-19.
2. Remfry, Leonard. "The Effects of Lactation on Menstruation and Impregnation," *Transaction of the Obstetrical Society of London*, Vol. 38, 1896 (London: Longmans, Green and Co., 1987). Available at www.nfpandmore.org.
3. Prem, Konald. "Post-Partum Ovulation," Unpublished research presented at the La Leche League World Conference, 1971. Available at www.nfpandmore.org.
4. Taylor, William et al. "Continuously Recorded Suckling Behaviour and its Effect on Lactational Amenorrhoea," *Journal of Biosocial Science*, 31 (1999) 296.

4

Fourth Standard

Sleep with Your Baby for Night Feedings

"Our last three babies slept with us for two years. Even though I'm 38 now and have a five month old, I've never felt tired like I did with our first one who slept in a crib in a separate room."

Nighttime nursings are important for maintaining a steady milk supply and for natural child spacing, and co-sleeping greatly assists both effects. Night feedings are normal for a breastfed baby. Many infants need one or several feedings nightly during the first few years of life. These form a normal part of the baby's nutrition. In fact, some doctors will be concerned for nutritional reasons if a small breastfed baby is sleeping during the night for a long time without nursing. What is noteworthy about co-sleeping is this: Babies who sleep next to their mother nurse three times longer during the night than those infants who sleep separately from their mother.[1] These frequent and unrestricted nighttime nursings are important for natural child spacing.

Extended breastfeeding infertility is associated with night feedings.

The mother who sleeps with her baby during the night is involved in a pattern of unrestricted breastfeeding. By taking care of her baby's needs for closeness, cuddling, and skin contact during the night, she also provides the opportunity for her baby to nurse as often as he pleases. In the Seventies a Chilean doctor confided to my husband that he encouraged mothers to cuddle their babies between their breasts during the night. This closeness stimulates the baby to nurse often and helps maintain the infertility of breastfeeding. This also happens when the baby is at the mother's side.

To show how sleeping with the baby influences the menstrual cycles, I would like to relate some true stories.

• Mother A had three babies who did not use pacifiers. The mother nursed exclusively during the early months and continued to nurse for one year. She sat up at night to nurse her babies and then placed them in a crib. By the fifth to sixth month postpartum, all three babies were sleeping through the night and her periods returned at 7 or 8 months after childbirth with each baby. With baby #4, she read my book on natural child spacing, bought a king-size bed and slept with her baby. She had her first period at 20 months postpartum while breastfeeding. Bedsharing made the difference.

• Mother B nursed her first baby who slept through the night. Her menstruation returned at 4 months postpartum. With baby #2, she slept with her baby and nursed throughout the night. She was still without any menstrual cycles at 21 months postpartum.

• Mother C weaned her earlier children between 3 to 7 months postpartum and her fertility soon returned. She decided to do ecological breastfeeding and sleep with her next baby. With eco-breastfeeding, her periods returned when her baby was 26 months old.

• Mother D had a very interesting situation with bedsharing. Her periods returned at 2 months after childbirth and occurred on a regular basis while breastfeeding her second baby. Her baby slept in another room, but that situation changed when her husband went on a business trip for three months. While he was gone, she brought her baby (now about 8 months old) and another child to bed with her. The baby nursed during the night and she had no menstruation for three months. Her husband returned home, the children left her bed, and she had some spotting the next month and observed the signs of returning fertility.

Working mothers

A few working mothers can experience a year of breastfeeding amenorrhea when they are gone all day but sleep with and nurse their baby throughout the night. One mother "day weaned" due to her busy home business, but allowed her baby to nurse during the night. In spite of her non-nursing during the day, her periods did not return until her baby was 19 months old due to bedsharing and night nursings.

The importance of night feedings

Since the first edition of *Breastfeeding and Natural Child Spacing* in 1969, more attention has been given to night feedings and their effect upon breastfeeding amenorrhea. Dr. Peter Howie, working with a research team in Edinburgh, Scotland, found that those nursing mothers who ovulated *earlier* nursed the least amount during the day, reduced the nursing times the fastest, introduced other foods quickly, and gave up the night feedings rapidly. On the other hand, the nursing mothers who ovulated *later* continued to give night feedings, nursed more often, introduced other foods slowly, and reduced their nursing times gradually. Dr. Howie concluded that "the effectiveness of suckling as an inhibitor of ovulation is certainly dependent upon breastfeeding practice. The resumption of ovulation may be dependent upon other factors as well, but certainly we would suggest that suckling is a major variable, if not ***the*** major variable in the control of postpartum ovulation and fertility" (emphasis in the original).[2]

Dr. Howie and his associates centered their work on the introduction of solids and the absence of night feedings, practices they felt undermined the amount and frequency of suckling and led to the return of ovarian activity. A contemporary American study found that among all nursing mothers who introduced other foods, the most important practice in delaying a return of their periods was nursing during the night.[3]

Twenty more cosleeping advantages for mother and baby:

1. Regular nursing during the night produces a regular supply of milk. This practice supports good breastfeeding.

2. Mother's presence stimulates her baby's breathing. Dr. Margaret Ribble explained that a mother's presence as her baby sleeps at her side "is a protection rather than a peril." She explains:

> The mother furnishes "the stimulus which is necessary to bring important reflex mechanisms into action. It so happens that the baby's first response to her touch is respiratory. From being held, fondled, allowed to suck freely and frequently, the child receives reflex stimulation, which primes his breathing mechanisms into action and which finally enables the whole respiratory process to become organized under the control of his own nervous system."[4]

3. Babies feel secure in the dark of the night when their mother is near. Bedsharing is one place where the trust begins that is needed for future relationships. The mother is present to her baby during the night as well as during the day.

4. A baby benefits because at night he can nurse to his full contentment in quiet, cozy surroundings. This is a time when his mother won't be interrupted, a time when he can use the breast to fulfill his suckling needs. It is known that babies at times will nurse on and off for several hours while mother sleeps. This is common in the older breastfed child as well.

5. This is another opportunity for the baby to receive immunities from his mother's milk if there's an illness in the home.

6. There may be no other place for the infant to sleep except with his mother. A public health nurse who had a conversion once she co-slept with her own baby regretted the times she insisted on a crib when visiting a poor family.

7. If there is a disaster or fire, baby is right there to be rescued. For the blind or disabled, this is an important point.

8. Mothers are usually more rested in the morning when they co-share sleep with their baby. No matter how often or how long the baby nurses during the night, the mother is generally rested in the morning and this restfulness is truly a big bonus for the entire family. The mother can function better and enjoy her family more when she is not tired.

9. Nursing is one job most mothers learn to do well in their sleep. If the mother cannot sleep, she can at least learn to relax and rest while she is nursing in bed. Most mothers co-sleep with their babies because it's easier and more convenient to do so.

10. Co-sleeping is an easy way to monitor a baby, especially during an illness. The rare time one of our babies had a cold I used an elevated infant seat in the middle of our bed to help our baby breath and sleep better.

11. UNICEF of the United Kingdom states:
Mothers take their babies to bed in order to breastfeed, comfort, settle and get to know their baby. Bedsharing encourages intimate contact between mother and baby which facilitates a close and loving bond. Successful breastfeeding and better sleep are more common among mothers and babies who share the same bed.[5]

12. Bedsharing makes for a quiet household during the night. Our children grew up in a family where a crying baby was rare. I have read several times that it is normal for a baby to cry several hours each day, and I cringe and want to say, "No, no, no!" Something is drastically wrong if a baby cries a few hours each day, but our society tells the parent that this is normal. Co-sleeping is usually a calm, peaceful event.

13. Burping the baby can be done in bed. For a newborn who might occasionally need to be burped during the night, the mother can remain in bed and place his upper body or chest up over her stomach, or she can turn sideways and place him partially over her hip.

14. With breastfeeding in bed the infant usually ends up sleeping on his back when he is finished. Breastfeeding almost automatically provides the "back" position recommended as a protective measure against Sudden Infant Death Syndrome (SIDS).

15. Mothers who claim to be the nervous type have noted the tranquilizing effect of breastfeeding. Nursing, besides putting baby to sleep, can also put the mother to sleep.

16. Bedsharing is convenient for both parents. No one has to get up during the night to attend to a baby. The mother is not resentful—the baby did not keep her up all night, nor did her

husband get to sleep through the night while she was up tending to and nursing the baby.

17. This practice eliminates a lot of decision making and possibly arguing between husband and wife. They do not have to decide who has to take care of the baby when he stirs or who will get up to warm the bottle. If the baby is already in their bed, the husband has another advantage—he doesn't have to get up to bring the baby to bed.

18. Dads often comment on how much they enjoy waking up with their baby nearby. With bedsharing the baby keeps in touch with his father as well as his mother.

19. For working parents—whether it is the father or the mother—it is one time that the baby can stay close to his mom or dad after having no contact with the parent during the day. I would strongly encourage working mothers to continue nursing so that they can enjoy this special closeness with their baby and easily care for their baby during the night without feeling fatigued in the morning.

20. Lastly, co-sleeping on a safe sleeping surface with breastfeeding and normal responsive parents is a practice followed in many societies throughout the world. In addition, breastfeeding reduces SIDS.

The safety of bedsharing in other countries

Co-sleeping has been done for years by mothers throughout the world. It is practiced in 90% of cultures. As Dr. James McKenna once said: "The culture is rare that doesn't sleep with their baby; breastfeeding and co-sleeping are functionally biologically interrelated."[6]

The risk of SIDS is very low in countries where bed-sharing among parents and little ones is common. Medical writer Lois Rogers listed some interesting statistics worldwide concerning SIDS and stressed that these deaths could be avoided or reduced by simply having the mothers sleep with their babies.

> "Leading scientists have found that unexplained infant death—when babies simply stop breathing and die in their sleep—is virtually unknown across 95% of the world, where infants generally sleep close to their mothers."[7]

Rogers states that SIDS is practically unheard of in India; among Asian babies 24 out of 25 sleep with their mother. In spite of poverty and overcrowding, these Asian babies have a much lower cot death rate than Britain where one-third of the babies sleep alone. In spite of the campaign for babies to sleep on their back in Britain, there are still between 400 to 500 cot deaths a year there. Britain's infant cot death rate or SIDS rate is 23 times higher than Hong Kong where bed-sharing is common.[8]

Another writer, Bill Manson, stressed two points: 1) that bed-sharing reduces SIDS and 2) babies would be happier and healthier if parents slept with their babies. Where it is customary for babies to share sleep with their parents (Hong Kong, Pakistan, Japan, and Bangladesh), the SIDS rates are very low compared to the United States, Britain, Canada, Australia and New Zealand where co-sleeping is uncommon. Manson showed how babies do not get smothered; healthy babies will scream the minute they get pinched or crowded.[9]

Bedsharing with little ones, even infants, is a practice that is done in many countries throughout the world. Studies consistently show that the baby sleeping in a separate bedroom apart from his parents is not the norm. In 79% of 127 societies studied, "infants normally slept in the same room as their parents, with 44% sharing the same bed or sleeping surface."[10]

Unfortunately, here in the United States many parents are taught by health-care professionals that the mother should never sleep with her baby and that the safest sleeping place for a baby is the crib.

On the contrary, medical and breastfeeding organizations report that breastfeeding reduces the incidence of SIDS, and evidence shows that co-sleeping enhances breastfeeding. Also, no place is 100% safe for any living person. Just by the fact that we are living means there is a risk of death, and that includes infants. There is no 100% risk-free sleeping environment for infants nor for adults.

Bedsharing likewise occurs in the United States where parents allow infants and older children into their beds, whether breastfeeding or not, due to parental fatigue or because their child wants to be there. It is better to teach parents how to share sleep safely with infants than to have the parents fear the crib because of crib deaths and to fear the parental bed because of fear-mongering messages from their community health professionals about not sleeping in bed with their baby. These parents then fall asleep with their baby on couches or other unsafe areas that increase the risk of SIDS to their babies.

Bedsharing positions

When breastfeeding in bed, mothers usually lie on one side facing the baby and have their arm extended above the baby's head, oftentimes with her elbow and legs bent. Her extended arm prevents her baby from moving up; her bent legs prevent her baby from moving down. This arm-and-leg position tends to keep the baby in one general area and reduces the risk of overlaying by the mother. As one mother said, "You couldn't roll over on the baby in that position without dislocating your shoulder."

We kept our baby or older baby in between us. The baby would nurse and at the same time reach towards his dad with his legs. I have always slept on the right side of our bed. When I nursed during the night, our baby was at my right side. The baby nursed on the right breast. Later I would rotate my upper chest so that the baby could nurse off the left breast without either one of us changing positions. My husband slept in the same bed with the baby and me.

Being so close to her child during the night, the mother can wake up temporarily at his first stir to offer the breast. The child does not have to stir and stir and then finally cry to get her attention as he would if he were in a separate room. If the dad first notices the baby mouthing or rooting for food during the night, he can tap mom on the shoulder. After offering the breast, the mother then dozes back to sleep. This becomes so easy and natural that a mother cannot say how many times she nursed during the night.

The American Academy of Pediatrics now encourages parents to respond to their babies before the crying begins. In their Breastfeeding Policy Statement one word was printed in boldface and italics. That word, "late," was used in the following sentence. "Crying is a *late* indicator of hunger."[11] Rooting, mouthing, and increased activity or alertness are the earlier signs of hunger to which parents should respond. With the family bed the mother can respond to these early signs of hunger during the night because of her physical closeness to her baby.

Some parents ask whether this practice will interfere with intimacy between husband and wife. At times of desired intimacy it is not necessary to bring the baby to bed until afterwards when you are ready to sleep. We kept our babies near us in the evening, even after the baby nursed to sleep. Our baby, sleeping or not, usually remained near us in the evening until we retired. Couples who want to engage in the marriage act can bring the baby to bed later.

In summary, if a baby wakes up at night because of a need that can be fulfilled at the breast, there is no easier and better way for the family to get back to sleep than to let the baby nurse at his mother's side in bed. This not only helps to satisfy the baby's nutritional and emotional needs, but it also satisfies the emotional needs of the mother. Not only is it restful for her, but she derives satisfaction in doing what is best for her baby and from having a contented and quiet baby as a result.

Safety guidelines for co-sharing sleep

Here are some safety guidelines you can follow for bedsharing:
- Breastfeed your baby exclusively. Breastfeeding decreases the risk of SIDS.
- Sleep only on a firm surface.
- Avoid a headboard and a footboard where your baby might get trapped between the furniture and the mattress. Or place the mattress on the floor.
- Use a king-size bed so there is room for you, your baby and spouse, or buy a sleep cot for the baby that attaches to the side of your bed.
- Keep soft comforters, pillows, siblings, pets, and stuffed toys away from your baby.
- Don't smoke and don't allow any smokers near your baby even if they are not smoking right then. Smoking is a very high risk factor for SIDS. A smoker's breath and body odors may be harmful to baby's breathing.

- Be sober. Any parent who sleeps with the baby should not drink heavily or take drugs or any medicine that will alter normal response.
- Don't overdress the baby so that he is too warm.
- Keep blankets and sheets away from the baby's head or upper body.

Regarding SIDS, sleep researcher Dr. James McKenna says, "The overwhelmingly majority of these deaths are attributed to a particular risk factor associated with bedsharing, such as maternal smoking, prone infant sleep, drug use, sleeping with other children, or sleeping on pillows or in beds with gaps into which the infants can fall and subsequently suffocate."[12]

Mississippi seeks to reduce its SIDS rate.
In the Delta region of Mississippi the SIDS rate was almost double the national average and was among the highest in the United States. Over 100 pieces of scientific literature were studied and discussed so the most effective means to reduce this problem could be determined. The result in 2001 was a three-prong educational approach:

1. Increase the proportion of infants sleeping in the nonprone position. Babies should sleep on their backs. Babies who sleep on their tummies are two to three times more likely to die of SIDS than those babies who sleep on their backs.

2. Decrease the proportion of young infants exposed to passive smoke in the home. Maternal smoking during pregnancy and after childbirth is "one of the significant predictors of SIDS." All parents and others around the baby should not smoke.

3. Increase the proportion of mothers initiating breastfeeding and continuing for at least 12 months. "Recent well-controlled studies have consistently shown that infants who were never breastfed were two or three times more likely to die of SIDS than their breastfed counterparts." Showing their awareness of the problem of overlaying with bedsharing, the researchers added: "However, *co-sleeping also results in increased breastfeeding and increased tactile stimulation (as a result of increased bodily contact), both of which are protective against SIDS*" (emphasis added).[13]

Parents want to protect their baby.

As a first-time mother, I had an extreme fear of harming our baby if I slept with her. Thus our first baby slept in a crib in another room in our small apartment. I would get up several times during the night to nurse her. Sometimes I fell asleep in the rocking chair nursing her during the night and would almost drop her. Mothers who nurse this way during the night may cause serious injury to their baby. I also limited the amount of nursing during the night since I was tired or cold and wanted to get back to bed as quickly as possible. This behavior limits the nursing and is not conducive to natural child spacing.

My fear of co-sleeping with my baby was eliminated after I unintentionally fell asleep nursing my second baby on top of the bedspread one afternoon. Three hours later I awoke and was surprised that the baby was nursing and I was so well rested. The actual "doing it" changed my mind.

In the mid-Sixties, I gave a presentation on breastfeeding to Canadian public health nurses. The nurses objected to my statements about the breastfeeding mother sleeping with her baby. After the session was over, the head nurse came up to me and apologized for the reaction of her nurses and said three things to make me feel better: 1) that she nursed her babies and slept with them, 2) that you don't accept this practice unless you've done it, and 3) it was a wonderful experience for her.

Since 1969 my husband and I have written about the benefits of co-sharing sleep between mother and baby because of our work with natural family planning. For natural child spacing, two of our rules dealt with the mother sleeping with her nursing baby for night and nap feedings. Between the years of 1969 and 2007, *Breastfeeding and Natural Child Spacing* sold about 90,000 copies, and *The Art of Natural Family Planning* sold about 400,000 copies. Both books promoted this practice. Not one parent in all those years ever contacted us and told us their baby died in bed with them.

Again, there is no risk free environment from death for our babies or for us. But it's time to have some sense about this practice. We have babies who die in their cribs or at daycare, but professionals are not telling parents: "Don't use cribs" or "Don't use daycare." I encourage you to have an open mind, read more

about this practice and decide for yourself as parents what you want to do or what you as a health-care provider would like your clients or patients to do. As one study concluded:
> The most current data support co-sleeping as the safest option when it is practiced in a safe and responsible manner by a sober, nonsmoking, and preferably breastfeeding mother on a safe surface. A similar statement, based on the most recent data, could be made for crib sleeping, that crib sleeping, when practiced in a safe, nurturant and responsible manner, provides a viable alternative to bedsharing when the parents are either unable or unwilling to safely bedshare or co-sleep with an infant. Not all parents can afford a crib. Not all parents can breastfeed or enjoy the "family bed."[14]

The oneness of mother and baby

Mother and baby are one biological unit after birth as they were before birth. It doesn't make sense for a mother to be one with her baby during the day and then be separated from her baby during the night. More information on co-sharing sleep and safety guidelines is available at "links" at www.nfpandmore.org, and several books and websites are devoted to this topic. Such books are available at breastfeeding websites.

I would like to conclude this topic with another quotation from Dr. James McKenna's "Co-sleeping and Overlaying" article available online.
> No infant sleep environment is risk free. As regards co-sleeping (in the form of bed-sharing) what we know to be true scientifically is that for nocturnal infant breastfeeding and nurturing throughout the night, both mothers and babies were designed biologically and psychologically to sleep next to one another...Infant-parent co-sleeping with nocturnal breastfeeding takes many diverse forms, and it continues to be the preferred "normal" species-wide sleeping arrangement for human mother-baby pairs. In the worldwide ethnographic record, mothers accidentally suffocating their babies during the night is virtually unheard of, except among western industrialized nations, but here there are in the overwhelming number of cases, explanations of the deaths that require reference to dangerous circumstances and not to the act itself.[15]

Natural aids to nursing during the night

It should be evident that the mother who adopts this natural mothering approach isn't going to be thinking in terms of getting her baby to sleep through the night. She will let the baby set the pace. But what if baby is an unusually heavy sleeper? There are several natural events that can help the mother nurse her sleeping baby at night.

One natural event is the desire by the mother to relieve her full breast. If the baby is an unusually heavy sleeper at first, she will want to encourage—not force—a nursing when she goes to bed and again when she first awakens. This relieves her breasts of excessive fullness and helps her maintain a steady milk supply and avoid plugged ducts. It is also a pleasant experience to nurse a sleepy baby at these times. The breast fullness seems to be nature's way of reminding the mother of her baby—and to be near her baby. It also helps the baby to get a regular intake of nourishment.

What if both mother and baby are such sound sleepers that the baby does not awake to nurse during the night? The biological fact of life is that eight hours without nursing may cause an early return of fertility. Is there anything a mother can do when this occurs without setting an alarm clock? Yes. She can drink a large glass of water before going to bed. After three to four hours, she will probably get a bladder wake-up call. Upon returning to bed, she can offer the breast to her sleeping baby.

A last word on breastfeeding infertility

If a mother anticipates that her breastfeeding will result in both a healthy baby and natural infertility, then she will not go 10 to 12 hours without nursing during the day. Likewise, she will not set a goal of going so many hours without nursing her baby during the night. The absence of feeding for any length of time may initiate an early return of her menstrual periods and thereby shorten her breastfeeding infertility. As stated earlier, research shows that the baby who sleeps next to his mother during the night nurses three times more than the baby who sleeps apart from his mother. If a mother wants the natural child spacing effect of breastfeeding, then sleeping with her baby and nursing him during the night is recommended.

Our little girl wakes at night to be nursed and sometimes nurses often at night. We have a king-size bed so it really doesn't bother our sleep. We have relied entirely on nursing for postponing pregnancy. It is the most enjoyable method of spacing babies. I just regret all the years that were completely safe or could have been and we didn't know it.

* * *

I believe not only in lying down while nursing but also in sleeping with one's children. My son nurses on and off during the nights. He is 22 months old and I have not yet had a period. Sleeping with one's children is so easy, so natural, so safe, and so warm and loving.

* * *

When we got our adopted baby, we put her right between us in bed from the very first night. That is a usual thing in many parts of the world. Adoptive parents are told that the baby may be used to sleeping with the foster mother. For us, sleeping with her really made the bonding fast. I think it makes her feel very secure. She likes to go to bed because she is with mom and dad.

* * *

I get the third degree about co-sleeping at each well check-up. At our last visit I got a little annoyed and finally replied that I have four children, have breastfed them all, and that Dr. James McKenna and Dr. William Sears have demonstrated through studies that co-sleeping can be done safely. Co-sleeping is a survival technique after an emergency c-section. If I didn't nurse lying down, it would be so painful to hold the baby near my incision. I'm convinced that many mothers give up breastfeeding because they do not get support from their husband, the medical profession, their church, and society.

1. McKenna, J., Mosko, S., and Richard, R. "Bedsharing Promotes Breastfeeding," *Pediatrics*, 100:2 (1997) 214-19.

2. Howie, Peter, "Synopsis of Research on Breastfeeding and Fertility," *Breastfeeding and Natural Family Planning,* Bethesda, Maryland: KM Associates, 1986.

3. Elias, M., et al., "Nursing Practices and Lactation Amenorrhea," *Journal of Biosocial Science,* January 1986.

4. Ribble, Margaret. *The Rights of Infants,* New York: Columbia University Press 1943, 1965, 18.

5. UNICEF of UK Statement on Mother-Infant Bed Sharing, February 18, 2004.

6. McKenna, James, Tri-State Breastfeeding Advocates Annual Conference for Health Professionals, Mason, Ohio, August 25, 2006.

7. Rogers, Lois. "Bed-Sharing May Cut Cot Deaths," *The Sunday Times,* October 8, 1995.

8. Ibid.

9. Manson, Bill. "Is Fatal Syndrome Halted When Babies Sleep With Mom?" *Washington Times,* December 26, 1993.

10. McKenna, J., Ball, H., and Gettler, L. "Mother-Infant Cosleeping, Breastfeeding and Sudden Infant Death Syndrome: What Biological Anthropology Has Discovered About Normal Infant Sleep and Pediatric Sleep Medicine," *Yearbook of Physical Anthropology,* 50 (2007) 136.

11. American Academy of Pediatrics, "Policy Statement: Breastfeeding and the Use of Human Milk," *Pediatrics,* 100:6 (December 1997). The same sentence appears in the revised AAP Policy Statement of the same title in *Pediatrics,* 115:2 (October 28, 2005) without the emphasis.

12. McKenna, James. *Sleeping with Your Baby,* Washington DC: Playpus Media, LLC, (2007) 70.

13. Kum-Nji, P., Mangrem, C., and Wells, P. "Reducing the Incidence of Sudden Infant Death Syndrome in the Delta Region of Mississippi: A Three-Pronged Approach," *Southern Medical Journal* 94:7 (2001) 704ff.

14. Morgan, H., et al. "The Controversy About What Constitutes Safe and Nurturant Infant Sleep Environments, *Journal of Obstetric, Gynecologic, & Neonatal Nursing,* November/December 2006, 684-689.

15. McKenna, James. "Cosleeping and Overlaying/Suffocation," Mother-Baby Behavioral Sleep Laboratory, www.nd.edu/~jmckenn1/lab/overlaying.html.

5

Fifth Standard

Sleep with Your Baby for a Daily-Nap Feeding

"Nursing lying down saved me. I was tired and tense, and I couldn't relax enough to nap. The solution: I nursed lying down after lunch. The baby fell asleep and the nursing hormones relaxed me enough to allow me to sleep. We're still nursing at 13 months postpartum and no menstruation yet."

Sleep with your baby for a daily-nap feeding. A daily nap refreshes a mother. She avoids fatigue which may affect or reduce her milk supply. The lack of a nap may also negatively affect the natural child spacing mechanism. The hormonal suppression of fertility is dependent upon lactation, especially good lactation involving frequent and unrestricted nursing. For those reasons I believe that a daily nap with the nursing baby is extremely important for most mothers in maintaining amenorrhea.

You may wonder how I arrived at these assertions. First, it is indisputable that a nap refreshes a mother—breastfeeding or not. Second, La Leche League has long counseled breastfeeding moms that fatigue can reduce her milk supply.[1] and I am sure such advice is based on thousands of woman-years experience. My third point, namely that the lack of a nap may negatively affect breastfeeding's natural infertility is inferred in two ways.

As you will see in the next chapter, breastfeeding's hormonal suppression of fertility is related to frequent and unrestricted nursing. With a nap, the mother has a time of unrestricted nursing and she becomes rested—both of which help to maintain a good milk supply.

The second inference comes from years of experience. When we receive a call from a mother stating that she is doing ecological breastfeeding but has had an early return of menstruation, one of the first questions we ask her is, "Are you taking a daily nap with your baby?" Almost always the answer is "no."

In the latter half of 1995 I analyzed the experiences of five mothers who had reported a return of menstruation from five weeks to four months postpartum while supposedly doing ecological breastfeeding. Four of the five early-return mothers did not take a daily nap with their babies. The mother who took daily naps with her baby discontinued them at eight weeks postpartum.

If a nursing mother is feeling pre-menstrual, she may postpone the return of menstruation if she can get more rest at night and also take a nap with her nursing baby. With more rest and a daily nap with her nursing baby, those pre-menstrual feelings may go away.

A nap should be a priority.

When we began our family in the 1960s, it was common for mothers, even my bottle-feeding friends, to take the phone off the hook and take a nap with their children during the afternoon. There were no answering machines then.

This custom of mothers napping with their children should be revived! I find mothers today rarely take a nap with their little ones on a regular basis, especially mothers with more than one child. Many mothers work and are not with their children during the middle of the day, and for them a nap with one's children is impossible.

Many mothers claim they are too busy, yet a short nap is so beneficial. Even UNICEF in 1999 used to say at their website for *Facts for Life: Breastfeeding*: "Breastfeeding can be an opportunity for a mother to take a few minutes of much-needed rest."

During the summer of 2007, I read three books on the benefits of taking a short nap during the day for young and older adults.[2] If a nap benefits this group, a nap would certainly be beneficial for the busy breastfeeding mother.

A short nap can recharge a mother's spirits. For years I have told mothers that babies are meant to slow mothers down. Mothers need that extra rest especially while breastfeeding. The main benefit of the daily nap is that moms usually have lots more energy toward the end of the afternoon and during the evening. They have a better disposition for handling anything that might come up later in the day.

Although some mothers have criticized this Standard as unworkable for a mother of many children, my own experience is the contrary. When I had a baby, a two year old, and a four year old, we all took a daily nap. All four of us would retire on our king-size bed. If the oldest one was not tired, I would tell her to lie there quietly for a half-hour. If she was still awake after a half-hour, she and I would get up. Oftentimes she fell asleep before the half-hour was over. With this policy I knew I would get at least a half-hour rest with three children.

I asked a friend, a mother of nine children, how she managed to get in a daily nap. She said she closed off a room in the house, any older child could not leave the room, only quiet toys were allowed for play, and she would lie on the floor nursing her baby in the same room.

In the old days kindergarten children were required to bring a rug to school. The children would lie on their rug at "rest" time. If a teacher could set aside "rest" time for the children in her class, certainly a mother should be able to set aside "rest" time as a priority for the little ones in her family. Rest benefits everyone. If an older responsible sibling is home, he can babysit while his mother rests with the baby.

I want to emphasize that taking a nap *does not mean* lying down to nurse the baby for his nap with the hope of getting up immediately to get things done as soon as the baby falls asleep. Taking a nap means the mother nurses and rests while doing so or she falls asleep for a short time while nursing her baby. She gets some much needed rest. **The goal is a short nap or rest for the mother while nursing her baby.** Thus unrestricted nursing is accomplished at the same time.

Personal experience without the nap

I experienced an early return (4½ months) with our fourth baby while getting a book ready for publication. Our breastfed baby was very alert, took brief naps, and did not sleep long in the evening until she retired with us. I used all my available time on the book, never took a nap, and simply did not get sufficient rest. The fatigue at that point in my life, I feel, was the reason for the early return of menstruation. Normal fertility, however, did not return until about 12 months postpartum, eight cycles later.

We can see from this and the experiences of others that even if an early return of menstruation has occurred, it does not necessarily mean that fertility has returned. However, if a mother wants to postpone pregnancy, she has to assume that a return of menstruation usually signals a return of fertility and so charting is recommended. Resources on charting or systematic natural family planning are available in Chapter 10. In any case, the return of menses can best be postponed by making a daily "nurse-nap" a priority.

Another mother's experience with naps

Here is the experience of a mother who found naps were not the answer with her first and second baby.

> If you remember, we had a colicky little girl and difficulties with nursing her and her older sister. Our first baby had some acid reflux and allergies, but now is a much happier baby. The "moby wrap" we bought was like a magic sleeping remedy. Whenever she was fussy and refused to sleep or nurse, I put her in our "kangaroo pouch" and she would settle down to sleep.
>
> Our almost three year old still nurses at night. We cut out naptime nursing because it was too frustrating and uncomfortable for me to nurse both of them and try to get them to sleep for naps by myself during the day. It just works better for our family and at 10 months postpartum I have still not had a return of my cycles.

Note that this mother did not take the daily nap and remained in amenorrhea at ten months postpartum. Some mothers will ignore this Standard of taking the daily nap and still experience an extended period of natural infertility. Other mothers may use a pacifier on a regular basis and still experience an extended period of natural infertility. Some mothers' bodies are more sensitive to the hormone-stimulating process of their baby's suckling and the mother remains in amenorrhea even though she may ignore one of the Standards.

In my studies, however, I found that many women need a lot of frequent and unrestricted nursing to keep the reproductive system at rest. I was one of them, a mother who required rest as well as frequent and unrestricted nursing to remain in amenorrhea during the first year of life. Though some have urged me to abandon my advocacy of a mother's daily nap feeding, I feel compelled to continue stressing the importance of following all of the Seven Standards for natural child spacing. I believe all Seven Standards are important for the majority of women. In and of themselves, the daily nap provides significant benefits to mothers and babies regardless of their effect upon the return of fertility. And for those mothers who need or want to space their babies solely through breastfeeding, the daily nap as described offers the greatest possibility of success.

How many naps do you have to take for breastfeeding infertility?

I am not aware of any studies that have related the number of daily naps to the duration of breastfeeding amenorrhea. Based on experience (personal and reports from others) as well as practicality, I recommend one nap of at least 30 minutes during the day. Usually the nap occurs during the middle of the day, such as after lunch. But a nursing mother who is very tired may choose to get back to bed with her baby in the morning. Likewise a new mother who just had a baby may need a short nap during the morning and again in the afternoon.

The key is for the mother to have an extended period of time during the day in which continuous and unrestricted suckling can take place. If the mom can sleep during this time all the better, but rest in any case truly helps.

Where do you take your nap?

Most mothers will use their bed, keeping in mind the safety guidelines for co-sharing sleep. I have also napped with a baby many times on the floor, a carpeted floor at that time. I also placed a firm comforter underneath us. The benefit of the "floor" situation is that the baby was nearby after I got up from my nap or rest. I preferred having the baby in my general area of activity. I was also near when the baby awoke. The main point is that you nap with your nursing baby where it's safe and where you can rest and relax.

It should be stressed that a mother should not "nap" with her baby on a couch or a chair. Studies show that these are not safe places for sleeping babies.

A daily nap can be very important.
Based on my experience with breastfeeding mothers who reported an early return of periods, I repeat that not taking that daily nap may be a key factor for some mothers who experience an early return of menstruation. Naptime nursing should not only provide sleep for the baby but should also provide sleep or at least a good rest for the mother. In that way naptime nursing helps to prevent or reduce fatigue; it also provides unrestricted nursing that produces strong hormonal surges in the mother's body at mid-day to help maintain amenorrhea after childbirth. It may also help to avoid any on-and-off spotting or sporadic bleeding. This is mentioned in one of the quotes at the end of this chapter.

Nursing your baby during a nap is an important practice to consider if you would like the natural baby-spacing effect of breastfeeding—especially in our culture where many mothers work and a mother who naps may feel guilty about not accomplishing anything while resting. There is nothing to feel guilty about when a mother exercises optimal self-care by allowing herself enough rest. This is good for the mother's physical and psychological health and, as such, benefits the baby. A rested mother is able to cope so much better with the vicissitudes of everyday life at home with young children than an exhausted one! As Dr. William Sears put it, "What a baby needs most is a happy and rested mother!"[3]

In summary, the unrestricted stimulation of the mother's breast from uninterrupted nursing during a daily mid-day nap may strongly influence her body chemistry toward natural infertility. A short daily nap just makes good sense with regard to natural infertility and, in my opinion, a daily nap facilitates better mothering.

> A daily nap is *good medicine* for the nursing mother. I had bouts of mastitis with two babies. I did not take any naps with these babies. With the third baby, I decided to take care of myself and the first step was to take that daily nap. As a result, I had no bouts of mastitis.

* * *

You asked me what I meant by "a daily nap making a difference." I found that prior to starting the daily-nap routine, my cycles/bleeding episodes were sporadic and un-period-like. That mean that the intervals between and the duration of the bleeding was unpredictable. Now, it seems like more of a period: the bleeding lasts 5 to 9 days, and the period does not return less than 4 to 5 weeks later. Maybe it is coincidental. At any rate, I am certainly more rested and energetic in the evening.

* * *

With our third baby I had not learned of the afternoon nap principle and I experienced my first menses at 9 months with a first fertile ovulation at 12 months based on temperature. With our fourth baby I began more-fertile mucus at 6 months and so I began taking an afternoon nap with her. The mucus declined and I didn't experience menses until 11 months postpartum with a first ovulation at 14 months.

We recently had our fifth. I was expecting to go a very long time without charting. At six weeks I had a bleeding episode that we attributed to hormonal bleeding. Much to my disappointment I had menses a day before our daughter turned 3 months old. I wasn't taking a daily nap with her. I began taking that daily nap with her, but I'm sad to think it may be too late. We have already begun charting. We love ecological breastfeeding. We have such happy babies as a result, but I wish I didn't have to worry about feminine supplies! Next baby I will not underestimate my need for the afternoon nap!

1. La Leche League International, *The Womanly Art of Breastfeeding*, 7th edition, (January 2004) 136, 319.
2. Anthony, William: *The Art of Napping*, Larson Publications, 1997; Long, Jill: *Permission to Nap*, Sourcebooks, Inc., 2002; Mednick, Sara and Ehrman, Mark: *Take a Nap!*, Workman Publishing, 2006.
3. Sears, William. L.A.T.C.H. conference, Chesapeake, VA. February 2002.

6

Sixth Standard

Nurse Frequently Day and Night and Avoid Schedules

"This is the only method of child spacing that appeals to my husband and me in every possible way. Myself, I look for simpler answers—ones that women in non-technological societies might discover—and in breastfeeding I found it."

Frequent nursing is common among eco-breastfeeding mothers. Doctor William Sears, author of many breastfeeding-related books, was once asked "How can a mother breastfeed successfully?" His answer was, "Frequently, frequently, and frequently." This same answer holds true for those mothers interested in the natural-child-spacing effect of breastfeeding: "Frequently, frequently, and frequently." It is the frequency of suckling that prolongs natural infertility after childbirth as well as helping a mother to nurse successfully.

Many breastfeeding mothers live in a culture where frequent breastfeeding is discouraged. Professionals, friends, family members, and authors of parenting books often tell mothers how to reduce the feedings within a short time after childbirth or give advice which leads to the same result of fewer feedings. This cultural advice is not helpful to the nursing mother who wants to do what is natural and best for her baby. Such advice tends to shorten both the duration of breastfeeding infertility and the duration of breastfeeding itself.

The frequency factor is research based.

The effects of breastfeeding frequency upon fertility were studied by James Wood, a research scientist at the University of Michigan's Population Studies Center. His subjects were a New Guinea people, the Gainj, whose breastfeeding episodes are short and frequent. In this culture, the child nurses on demand day and night, and he always sleeps with his mother. He begins solids at about nine to twelve months of age and completes his weaning at or near his third birthday.

Dr. Wood and his team carefully recorded the frequency of nursings and the intervals between nursing sessions. With their infants, the Gainj mothers averaged 24 minute intervals; with their three-year-olds, they averaged about 80 minutes between nursings. The important thing is that the reduction in suckling frequency occurred very slowly. The research team concluded, "The finding that suckling frequency is high and changes only slowly over time appears to be of special importance in explaining the prolonged contraceptive effect of breastfeeding in this population."[1]

The demographic picture demonstrates the spacing value of breastfeeding among this people who do not practice contraception or abortion. Their average birth interval was 44 months with an average family size of 4.3 children. The researchers explained that if these Gainj women abandoned breastfeeding, the number of live births would more than double per woman. As the researchers concluded, "the reproductive consequences of breastfeeding in this population are profound."

The !Kung tribe of Kalahari Desert in southern Africa has mothering and breastfeeding frequency patterns similar to those of the Gainj people. (The ! in !Kung represents a tongue-clucking sound.) Researchers Konner and Worthman found that !Kung women were *conceiving* on the average of 35 months postpartum, thus having an average birth interval of 44 months, the same as the Gainj mothers. They also observed that among this non-contracepting people the little one remained physically close to his mother day and night during the first two years. !Kung babies nursed several times each hour for just a few minutes each time. Konner and Worthman concluded that the frequency factor was the likely key to the child spacing of these people.[2]

Nursing one's baby several times during the hour seems to be the norm, according to Dr. R. V. Short. He referred to two groups of hunter-gatherers: the !Kung tribe just mentioned and another tribe in Papua, New Guinea, where mothers also nurse frequently. He thinks that "the biochemical composition of human milk, which is low in fat, protein and dry matter" fits into the need for frequent suckling. While "this high frequency of suckling may seem abnormal at first," Dr. Short holds that frequency is probably nature's norm. Even the chimps and the gorillas (the human species' closest relatives) suckle several times an hour in the wild, sleep with their babies, and have birth intervals of four to five years---similar to the two previously mentioned primitive tribes. Dr. Short credits the frequent suckling stimulus as "the crucial factor in causing the contraceptive effect" of breastfeeding.[3]

We have discussed the breastfeeding habits of certain tribes. What about mothers in developed countries? Many mothers in developed countries, such as America, are not accustomed to the frequent nursing of the previously mentioned tribes. Would they get similar results if they breastfed in a more traditional manner by following the Seven Standards?

H. William Taylor, Ph.D., worked with a group of breastfeeding mothers who would be more inclined to follow more of the mothering practices typical of traditional breastfeeding cultures. The 72 American mothers in the study averaged 14 months of postpartum infertility.[4] Dr. Taylor's research reaffirmed a very important conclusion for natural child spacing: what is important for breastfeeding infertility is **short intervals between feedings**. Those mothers who nursed frequently with shorter intervals between feedings were more likely to ovulate later. Those mothers who nursed with long feedings and long intervals between feedings tended to ovulate earlier.

What is important to point out here is that both groups of mothers—those who nursed with shorter intervals between feedings and those who nursed with longer intervals between feedings—nursed about the same amount of time during the 24-hour day. Yet only one behavior, short intervals between feedings, was associated with delayed ovulation. Dr. Taylor's study also showed that those mothers who scheduled their nursing sessions, introduced other liquids early, and left their baby alone at an early age ovulated earlier. These three behaviors meant that the breastfeeding sessions occurred further apart so that there were more hours between feedings, and thus the spacing achieved through breastfeeding was lost. The lesson is clear: the shorter the intervals between feedings, the more the natural child spacing effect is enhanced.

A few babies are not frequent nursers.
Occasionally a mother will write saying her baby does not want to nurse frequently. She blames this lack of interest in nursing for an early return of menstruation, or sometimes the mother is surprised that she is still in amenorrhea. This latter situation is described below.

> Nursing Lisa has been a beautiful experience. She is a wonderful, contented baby. Her weight gain has been well above normal. She gave up that 2:00 a.m. feed very early at six weeks. At three months she gave up the 10:00 p.m. feed, so I had that long stretch without nursing at night again. I went back to night feedings but she gave up one of her daytime feedings so I was still on four feeds a day. I spasmodically fed her at night but it was obvious she did not want it. I finally gave up and she seemed happier. At six months she went to three feeds a day with four every now and then. I began solids around 5½ months with small pieces of banana and gradually introduced other foods. Lisa was ready for solids and took to them greedily. I always nursed her before solids.
>
> Now she eats three meals a day and I cut out her midday nursing. However, she has been sick, and the last three nights with high fever she has gone back to nursing since nothing else makes her happy. One would expect a return of periods and/or ovulation with such a decrease in nursing, but apparently I must be able to keep the levels of inhibitory hormone high enough to prevent ovulation.

Such infrequent nursing usually means a return of fertility. However, there are some women as noted above who remain in amenorrhea with such few nursings. I have an acquaintance who is super-sensitive to any nursing. If she is nursing, no matter how little the amount, she remains in amenorrhea. She also has a friend with the same experience. This is not unusual for these breastfeeding mothers. However, it should be noted that for most mothers, frequent stimulation is the norm for breastfeeding infertility.

Be assertive if you live in a bottle-feeding culture.

For successful breastfeeding, you should not be discouraged from nursing frequently. Frequency is a desirable goal. Limiting the nursing through schedules and other means is not a goal for successful breastfeeding and natural child spacing.

In many societies where bottle-feeding is the norm, nursing mothers feel compelled to express milk in a bottle or use formula when they are away from home. Some mothers have noticed a return of menstruation after visiting relatives over the holidays. They found themselves in an environment unfavorable towards breastfeeding, and they reduced their nursings considerably.

Many societies discourage public nursing, *even modest public nursing*, or nursing outside the family circle so that most people never see a baby at the breast. If they have seen a baby nurse, most likely the baby was their brother or sister or a very close relative's. I married at age twenty-three, and up to that time I had never seen a mother nurse her baby.

If you want to do ecological breastfeeding with unrestricted nursing in a society where this type of breastfeeding is often unwelcome, you need determination. You can learn how to nurse modestly anywhere and to nurse comfortably in various social situations so you do not need to reduce your nursings. As your baby continues to nurse frequently with age, you will learn to be more comfortable with this continued pattern as well. The studies I have quoted reinforce what I have learned from personal experience and from other nursing mothers—namely, that with long-term nursing the frequency continues for an extended period of time and gradually diminishes toward the time of complete weaning. Usually the frequency of nursing is such that a mother hardly notices any changes in the frequency because the change is usually so gradual or the changes occur toward the end of the breastfeeding relationship. Whatever pattern the baby grows into as he ages, eventually he does wean.

It may sound as if all a mother does is nurse her baby. This is a false picture, although there are a few exceptions—especially during the early months. I have heard a few mothers say their babies required constant nursing during the early postpartum weeks. This is unusual, though, and not the norm.

With ecological breastfeeding, a baby nurses frequently but the feedings are usually brief. The long feedings usually occur when a baby is upset or hurt—which usually isn't often—and when he is tired prior to falling asleep. Some of these "tired" times are no inconvenience because you can also sleep when your baby is tired during your nap and during the night. You can reassure yourself from the research and the experience of other nursing mothers that your baby's frequent nursing pattern is normal and is the type of breastfeeding and mothering associated with extended postpartum infertility and many health benefits for you and your baby.

> We have been engaged in ecological mothering—enjoying not only the natural infertility as planned by God but also the wonderful closeness and bonding that can only be achieved by such a relationship.

* * *

> I thank you for the positive effect you've had on my mothering skills. I nursed my first baby for 4 ½ months and then quit because of the inconvenience. I nursed my second baby for 22 months because it was so very convenient. The only thing that changed was my attitude and finding a supportive group of friends.

* * *

> There are those mothers who believe the best thing for their babies is to be taught to be a 'good baby' whereas I believe my babies will teach me to be a good mother. I think these mothers are sincere in trying to do what is best, although from

my perspective that seems to be doing what is most convenient.

1. Wood, J. "Lactation and Birth Spacing, *Journal of Biosocial Science*, Supplement, 9 (1985) 159.
2. Konner, M. and Worthman, C. "Nursing Frequency, Gonadal Function, and Birth-Spacing Among !Kung Hunter-Gatherers," *Science* (February 15, 1980) 788.
3. Short, R. "Breast Feeding," *Scientific American* (April 1984) 35.
4. Taylor, W., Smith, R., and Samuels, S. "Post-Partum Anovulation in Nursing Mothers," *Journal of Tropical Pediatrics* (December 1991) 286-292.

7

Seventh Standard

Avoid Any Practice that Restricts Nursing or Separates You from Your Baby.

"He comes with me everywhere. I enjoy taking him with me. I could not leave him as it would be like amputating a limb and leaving it behind."

Nature intends for mother and baby to be one, a biological unit. Mothers who remain with their babies will find it easy to follow the eco-breastfeeding program. Nature rewards the eco-breastfeeding mother by providing many benefits to her, including natural child spacing. Any mother who is interested in natural mothering and its related child spacing effect should desire the oneness that nature intended between mother and child. In fact, such a mother soon discovers that she does not want to leave her baby; instead she makes every effort to have her baby with her no matter where she goes.

The World Health Organization described this oneness well: "Mothers and babies form an inseparable biological and social unit; the health and nutrition of one group cannot be divorced from the health and nutrition of the other."[1] Other researchers have described mother and infant as one biological system.

Mother-baby togetherness is the key to natural child spacing.

The practice of mother-baby togetherness has an impact on natural child spacing. The following example helps to make this point. A study conducted in the West African country of Rwanda discovered that there were no differences in the birth intervals of *bottle-feeding* mothers in the city compared to those in the rural areas. On the other hand, among *breastfeeding* mothers, there were significant differences. The city breastfeeding mothers were already developing patterns of separation from their babies; 75% of the city breastfeeding mothers *conceived* between 6 and 15 months postpartum. However, in the rural areas, the breastfeeding mothers still kept their babies with them all the time; 75% of the rural breastfeeding mothers *conceived* between 24 and 29 months postpartum. In this culture there were no contraceptives used or taboos against intercourse after childbirth. The researchers concluded that the only difference they could see between the two breastfeeding groups was the amount of physical contact the baby had with his mother.[2]

The mother is important.

A chief ingredient for a healthy start in life is the presence of a continuous loving relationship with one mother figure. Nature has ensured this loving consistent caring from the mother through breastfeeding. Eco-breastfeeding provides lots of "mother" contact for the baby and is eminently well suited for taking care of baby's nutritional and emotional needs.

With breastfeeding the importance of the mother to her baby becomes even more evident. Maria Montessori was a strong promoter of breast-milk-only for the first six months of life, very gradual weaning, and mother-baby inseparability during the early years. In fact, she recommended nursing for 1½ to 3 years. Why? Because "prolonged lactation requires the mother to remain with her child."[3] She had it right back in 1949 when she wrote the first edition of *The Absorbent Mind*. Where would societies be today if parents had listened and followed her advice?

The oneness of mother and baby is important for society.

How can we improve society? William Gairdner in his book, *The War Against the Family*, claims that there is unanimity on this important point: **"*poorly attached children are sociopaths in the making.*"**[4] To avoid poorly attached children, the answer is good mothering. His key words for good mothering are these: availability, responsiveness, and sensitivity. Mr. Gairdner pointed out that three separate research studies conducted at three different major universities all clearly showed that what babies and young children need is 1) mother's availability, 2) mother's sensitivity to her child's signals, and 3) mother's responsiveness to her child's need for comfort and protection. In other words, the mother has to be there, she has to read the signals of her baby, and she has to respond to her baby in a sensitive manner.

Gairdner also states that "young children need an uninterrupted, intimate, and continuous connection with their mothers, especially in the very early months and years."[5] With prolonged breastfeeding, the mother does have an uninterrupted and continuous relationship with her baby, and it's an intimate relationship as well.

Andrew Payton Thomas in his book, *Crime and the Sacking of America*, believes that one of the reasons the crime rates are soaring is because both parents are joining the workforce.

> The rise of daycare in modern America says some painful things about us as parents and as a nation and culture, things that are easier for adults to leave unsaid. But the truth is always worth telling, and it is this: Many American parents today simply do not wish to raise their own children. Indeed, never before in history have a people become so intensely individualistic that their love for their children can be purchased so cheaply... Children are taught, literally from the cradle, that life is looking out for #1.[6]

Gerald Campbell, head of The Impact Group, claims that the #1 problem in our society is alienation, an emptiness, "an aloneness that cannot be tolerated by the human heart." What people really need in his estimation is love, understanding, mercy and compassion, and commitment" from **one** person who learns to give of self "without any conditions or expectations whatsoever."

He spoke of daycare as the ill of the future, and he stressed the value of a mother's presence.[7]

To prevent alienation in our society and to develop healthy individuals who feel loved and valued, good care by the mother for her child during the first three years of life is crucial. What is so important about breastfeeding is that it usually gives babies the best nurturing and the best nutrition. Prolonged lactation naturally provides those two realities that make such a positive difference!

1997 was a year of studies for the infant.

The United Nations General Assembly proclaimed 1997 as the International Year of the Child. Since these designations are made years in advance, there was ample time for research. Thus 1997 was a famous year for such publications.[8] In the spring of 1997, new studies showed that "the neurological foundation for problem solving and reasoning are largely established by age one" and that the "number of words an infant hears each day from an attentive, engaged person is the single most important predictor of later intelligence, school success and social competence."[9] These studies stimulated new interest in the effects of nurturing and breast milk upon the brain. As a result, *Newsweek* published an entire issue on "the critical first three years of life."[10]

The main conclusion of the 1997 studies was that the number of words a baby hears during the first year of life must come from an "attentive, engaged human being." Discussion centered on the importance of the parents' role in the intellectual development of their child during the first three years of life and especially the first year of life when the infant's brain is growing at a tremendous rate. By nature, that engaged, attentive person is the breastfeeding mother.

In the fall of 1997 there was another series of studies dealing with maternal deprivation. At the Society of Neuroscience meeting in New Orleans, it was reported that children need lots of hugs and physical reassurance for proper development of the brain. Romanian children raised without this physical contact from their mother had abnormally high levels of stress hormones. This parental neglect can have lifelong consequences. "Scientists have known for decades that maternal deprivation can mark children for life with serious behavioral problems, leaving them withdrawn, apathetic, slow to learn, and prone to chronic illness. Moreover, new animal research reveals that without the attention of a loving caregiver early in life, some of an infant's brain cells simply commit suicide."[11] Does this apply to humans? Mark Smith, a psychologist at the DuPont Merck Research Labs in Wilmington, Delaware said: "These cells are committing suicide. Let this be a warning to us humans. The effects of maternal deprivation may be much more profound than we had imagined."[12]

How does stress affect the child's brain? How does a mother's presence protect or minimize the effects of stress upon her baby's brain? During stress the body secretes large doses of cortisol to provide strength. However, cortisol can also shrink the hippocampus, the part of the brain responsible for learning, and can stunt the brain cells' ability to communicate with each other by causing the connecting dendrites to atrophy. This helps to explain why cortisol is associated with severely delayed development. That's the bad news. The good news is that the mother's physical contact with her baby protects the baby against these harmful effects.

There are not many in Westernized cultures today who promote the importance of the mother being there for her baby during the early years. One does not want to offend the many mothers who seek fulfillment at the office or the classroom. In addition, many societies keep telling mothers that anyone can replace them. But that's not true. A mother should be irreplaceable in the early life of a child. Today one hardly ever hears or reads what the experts and studies have shown, that it's the concentrated interaction with one parent during the first three years of life that is so important. It's because the baby is so important that the mother's presence is so important. With prolonged lactation the mother can give many, many hours of nurturing during the crucial first three years.

There is no reason to leave your baby at home.
In a bottle-feeding culture babysitters are frequently used so mother can leave her baby. Some nursing mothers express their own milk for this reason. The same holds true for those dedicated

nursing mothers who simply cannot avoid employment outside the home. If the breastfeeding mother has to work, she will hopefully make every effort to cut back on her hours or to try to work either part-time, or at home, or with her baby. It is sad in a bottle-feeding society when a breastfeeding mother has to de-bond from her baby prior to returning to work so her baby will not miss her and will take a bottle during her absence. Support in bottle-feeding societies for mother-baby togetherness is a rarity.

Separations of parents and baby are common in our society, even long separations of one or two weeks. A friend of ours expressed dismay when she learned we always included the children in our trips. She informed me critically that getting away by yourselves as a couple once or twice a year was necessary if you wanted to have a happy marriage. This is exactly what they did. Yet, sad to say, their marriage ended in divorce years later. Both my husband and I feel that the goal shouldn't be to get away from your children, especially when they are extremely young. Our first two children were about one and three years old when she offered us this advice. We feel the goal should be to maintain your closeness as a couple without leaving your children.

I might also add that my parents always included my sister and me on all trips and vacations. But my husband remembers being excluded from some of his parents' trips as a small boy, and these were not good experiences. This is one area where he wishes his parents had done it differently. So because of past experiences for both of us, leaving the children at home for vacations was never a consideration.

It is becoming more popular for couples to vacation without their babies. Remember that babies have no concept of time. They have no idea where you are or when you will return. Parents, especially the mother, should have bonded with her baby. If so, the baby should miss her dearly. Usually the nursing intensifies the bonding. Imagine how you would feel if your spouse left one day and you did not hear from him at all for one or two weeks. You had no idea why he left nor did you know when he would return. Most of us in this situation would be concerned, upset, maybe mad, and hurt. That's similar to the feelings of a "deserted" baby.

A mother writes about attending a three-day seminar and her baby's reaction to the separation:

> I decided to attend a technical seminar for three days when Clare was 17 months old. This meant I was away from her from 7 to 9 hours per day. I wasn't worried about leaving her since my parents were coming down to watch her and she was able to go that long without nursing. It was while I attended this seminar that I found out the primary benefit of mother-baby togetherness.
>
> The first morning of the seminar I nursed Clare in bed as usual. After she finished she did her typical hugging and caressing me. All I could think of was how hard it would be to leave her. Clare got along great with my parents and I had an enjoyable time at the seminar, so much so that visions of going back to work full-time danced in my head. However, what really made me reconsider this was how Clare treated me after the seminar was over. She still nursed as often as usual, but the hugging and caressing had stopped. Not only that but at times she even preferred to play with my mother rather than with me. I thought what it would be like to have Clare be more responsive to a total stranger (i.e., a babysitter I'd have to hire) rather than her own mother. Fortunately, the seminar did not totally shatter our relationship. After spending an entire day with Clare, the loving relationship continued where it left off.

With eco-breastfeeding there simply will be times when you cannot go with your husband on a business or social trip. My husband made two trips to Rome when I could not go because of our young children. No one seemed to understand why I stayed home. But my husband understood and was very supportive, even though being in Rome without his wife was definitely lonely for him. I have known of couples who turned down rewards of free vacations because their baby was not allowed. But let's not forget the advantages: ease in traveling for the mother anywhere with her breastfed baby whether it's hiking, camping, touring, or visiting.

Mother-baby togetherness is a practice that usually produces happy mothers and happy babies. The mother's presence is what makes the baby so content! Mothers who practice ecological breastfeeding discover they want to be with their babies because separations are painful. The mother tries to avoid such separation. She enjoys her baby and keeps him with her.

Some mothers have noticed improved changes in their children's behavior once they decide to try the natural mothering program and its associated philosophy of being in tune with their child's needs. The following two true examples illustrate the need for children to have this special physical loving closeness with their mother.

> "Our son is in the terrible-two stage at this time and we seem to be always yelling and spanking him. The past two days I have catered to his wants totally, and my husband remarked how affectionate and well behaved he seemed to be and asked jokingly if he were sick. He is not aware of my reading your book or a change in my attitude. Things go much smoother now, even though I am doing what others would consider spoiling him."

> "I wanted to say that from my experience as a daughter and mother, natural mothering is the only way to raise children. My father (a doctor) never let my mother get close to me for fear of having a momma's baby, even telling her to give up nursing since I cried more often than every three hours. I feel that idea has hurt our relationship today. I am not able to be open to them and confide in them.
>
> As a mother at 19, I tried to follow the typical advice about formulas and schedules and potty training, and became a very frustrated mother to the point of shaking and spanking my child. After four more babies I gradually changed. I nursed the last one and really learned how to enjoy all of them. As for my parents, they were ready to pack their bags and go home once when I tried to rock and hold our eight year old while she was having a temper tantrum. Thanks for listening."

Breastfeeding provides a wonderful opportunity for physical contact between mother and baby. For those parents who fear they may hurt their children physically or abuse them verbally and become excessively angry with their children, breastfeeding is an excellent way to learn patience and strive to be that better parent.

Better parenting

A friend told me she hit her previous babies or little ones often, but with breastfeeding her behavior changed and she found this "hitting" behavior stopped. She gave credit to this change in her behavior to breastfeeding. A close friend had a relative who was very neglectful of her other children, so much so that my friend had to make sure the children ate breakfast and got to school in time. But the mother was not neglectful when she was breastfeeding. Breastfeeding changed her behavior for the better. Another mother confided to me that she wanted to wean her baby, but he insisted on still nursing. She later found out that he was abused at daycare and was so thankful she had listened to her baby and had continued to nurse him.

Many mothers have reported their appreciation of breastfeeding and how much it influenced their mothering for the better. For me, I think about this now and then when I receive a phone call from one of my grown children and their conversation generally ends with "I love you." Why do I say this? I came from a family where my mom and dad were always home. I knew they loved me but they never said it or showed it physically. In those days we didn't hear a lot about relationships or about the importance of having a mom and a dad living in the same home. My mom told me she never rocked me or did the things I did for my babies. Yet she was there. Dad was there. Toward the end of their lives as they needed more care and attention, I was able to say to them, "I love you," something I was not able to do when I was growing up as a child. And I credit that change to the breastfeeding relationship I had with my children.

Sometimes mother-baby togetherness can influence other mothers; it becomes contagious. One mother relates this experience:

> I nursed my first baby for 4½ months (three months exclusively), but considered it a nursing failure. The baby did not gain well on breastfeeding alone as I used schedules and no lying-down nursing. Our second was nursed frequently—about every two hours for the first year, slept with us, and went everywhere with us (including conventions, weddings, parties, meetings, and restaurants). Our emotional bond is much different and I really enjoyed this baby. As a result of

our example, at least three of our friends with previously bottle-fed, baby-sat babies are now following natural mothering and loving it. Having our happy, well-behaved baby with us all the time has been a joy, and many people have remarked on this.

Mother-baby togetherness is not always easy.

Some mothers have a small child who seems to need his mother all the time. The following letter shows that good things happen when a mother tries to meet those needs generously.

My fourth child had an unusually intense need for my physical presence. His need to have me available to meet his needs was very intense and long-lasting. He was so possessive of my attention that I really felt I ended up neglecting my other children (let us not even consider the housework!). I had to pour everything I had into meeting his needs. This baby would not let me out of his sight. I tried to leave him with his father from time to time, but was unable to do so until he was 18 months of age. He either went with me or I didn't go.

I was glad that I had three other more normal children because this baby was constantly on my body for the first 18 months of life. I used a carrier exclusively. I really needed the support my La Leche League group offered me, even though I knew I was doing the right thing by meeting all his needs. We left him with his grandmother about two times a year until he was two.

All the rest of society told me there was something wrong with me to produce such a dependent child, and there was something wrong with him for being that way. In brave moments I would just laugh and tell them that I expected great things from Joe, that the love you invest in children is returned to you and the world a thousand-fold when they mature, and I had poured more love into Joe than any other child on earth. Joe reached the independence of the average 18-month-old when he turned three. We debated about sending him to school when he came of age. Obviously he was unable to stand the separation of school during the pre-school years. When he turned six, he reached another new level of independence and started the first grade the very next month very happily.

At the time of this writing, Joe is seven years old, and

quite the most self-assured, independent, loving, thoughtful child you have ever seen. I know God has a plan for Joe. I'm glad I met his needs when he was a baby. I never could have done so without the support of *Breastfeeding and Natural Child Spacing*. I feel confident that if I had been unwilling or unable to meet his needs he would have been a very different person, equally as angry and evil as he now is happy and good.
Thanks from all of us.

As this mother has shown, much of the happiness in life and in parenting comes from helping others, especially our children. Being human, we all have to work at developing certain virtues, even when breastfeeding. No one is naturally good or loving. Most of us have a tendency to think mostly of ourselves. It is a continual effort to put ourselves at the service of others and to develop better traits. Breastfeeding helps a mother to mature and to develop as a giving person in a very gradual and easy manner. Breastfeeding cannot guarantee that our children will turn out well, but it can become a learning process whereby a new mother begins to think of others and to develop certain caring virtues that will hopefully help her during her later mothering years.

Babies do want to be near their mother.
Some mothers have reported that their babies cry when nursed to sleep and placed in a crib or in an area away from the mother. Some babies cry upon awakening when they find themselves alone and mother is nowhere in sight. These situations are usually eliminated when the mother changes her attitudes and keeps the baby near her. Where the mother goes, the baby goes. Where mother is, the baby is. Isn't that a simple rule to follow? The baby who is always in close proximity to his mother is a very secure baby.

Mothers want support for eco-breastfeeding.
Probably the most difficult emotional factor in mother-baby inseparability is finding friends who feel the same way about parenting, especially mothering. As one mother said, "Having to cope with criticism from the grandparents who feel our daughter should be weaned or that we pay too much attention to her makes things difficult on occasion." Or: "The most difficult aspect of

mother-baby togetherness involves taking our baby along to some events at which she is not really welcome. It's hard to find friends who share the same values that you do." Or: "The first few times I left the baby with her father or sitter proved to be pretty traumatic for her and me alike. I don't know who missed whom more. Even now I have a tendency to put off getting a sitter for a night out because there is still some separation anxiety for both of us." Most mothers who have done eco-breastfeeding have experienced some or all of these feelings. Yet in spite of these difficulties, parents keep saying they realize they are doing the right thing. As one mother wrote:

> Our baby went everywhere with us. He attended weddings, parties, meetings, and peace rallies. Now at 15 months he is very active, happy and friendly. He still goes almost everywhere with us, but once in a while we can leave him with friends for a couple of hours to take in a movie. He seems secure with this and does just fine. As for natural mothering, we would do it all over again. It does take support of like-minded friends and a dedicated spirit.

What's required on the part of the mother is a change in attitude.

In our society this "togetherness" practice takes some readjustment in thinking. I know it did for me. I went from "Where am I going and who will I leave the baby with?" to trying to leave only when the baby was asleep and returning when necessary for a nursing. The final change came when I took the baby or toddler or small child with me everywhere, no matter what others thought. Even if the baby was asleep, I picked up the baby and went.

The same philosophy can be applied at home. Running downstairs to do the laundry or upstairs to make a bed does not have to separate you from your child. You simply bring him with you. When the small one falls asleep (usually nursing to sleep), keep the sleeping child right in the area where you will be. This means that the baby is not sleeping in a room separated from your activity or in a room secluded upstairs away from the household activity.

Even an older baby or preschooler enjoys mother's presence while falling asleep at night. Dad may also be an acceptable substitute as the child grows in age. This is a good time to end the day and to make the child feel good about himself if things did not go well that day. Parents can use bedtime with their children for reading, quiet singing, praying and storytelling. There are ways to end the day without using videos, television, or recorded music to help a child go to sleep.

Child etiquette

When they're away from home, parents should always consider the occasion and the feelings of others who might be present. We went to a special annual banquet and were disappointed to learn that nursing babies were not allowed. The reason given was that the previous year a mother brought her nursing baby, and her baby cried the entire evening. The audience could not hear the speakers. That mother was not considerate of others, and as a result other nursing mothers were barred from future events. Nursing mothers need to realize that when they attend a meeting or a talk they may have to leave the room because their baby is fussy or crying. They can return when the baby has settled down.

Natural mothering does not mean permissive mothering. When you are in public places, take care of your baby and be considerate of others.

Separations

An older nursing baby can usually begin to take brief separations from mom, such as an hour or two at the most, especially if he is having a good time at home or if he likes his caregiver. These brief separations can begin sometime after the child's first birthday, but the time varies when a child willingly accepts these separations of an hour or two.

Children find it easier to accept separations of one or two hours during the daytime and early evening than at night. Upon your return, you may find the babysitter or your husband or older children telling you that your child was just beginning to miss you. Our last two children experienced their first separation of about one and a half hours at 15 and 18 months respectively. The occasion was their parents' decision to have dinner out alone but close to home. The 15 month old started missing me before I returned; the 18 month old hardly knew I left. When I left the latter child the first time for a full day at a local conference, he was five years old and showed no signs of distress that day. However, for the next few days he would not let me out of his sight.

I don't want mothers to set any goals by my babies, nor do I want to have mothers feel guilty for leaving their children at home. You and your child can communicate and work these things out together. If you try a brief separation and it doesn't work, then you might wait a while before you try again. Once separations do begin, they should be infrequent at first with a lot of consideration given to the child and his reaction to any separation.

Nighttime separations can be much harder for a child under two years of age. A child who has been nursed as described in this book may at 18 months choose to stay home with dad while mother runs to the store during the daytime. But this same child may have a strong need to be near mother at night. We accepted this fact, mainly from past experiences, and took our younger children with us everywhere in the evenings (be it social, for meetings, or for classes we taught) for their first two years of life. When they turned two, after a few explanations and discussions, each child would decide if he or she was big enough to stay home for the two or three hours we would be gone. Even then, we would occasionally come home to a child staring out the window waiting for our return. Sometimes the older siblings pretended they were talking to me on the phone so they could tell the youngest that mom would be home soon.

Nighttime separations are easier to handle when the older children or the babysitter understand the situation and are therefore very helpful in keeping him occupied with play or books. If one nighttime separation is hard on your child, then bring him with you the next time. That's what we did. Most two year olds soon decide that adult company and meetings are boring and decide to stay home at night on their own.

Sometimes bringing a babysitter along with you and with your child or children is a good alternative to separation. For example, when our first three children were 2, 4, and 6 years old, we played tennis at a park where the playground was across a busy street from the courts. So we could play tennis without worrying about the children, we hired a neighborhood girl to come with us and watch them at the playground. This way we all had a good time.

We found a similar situation while teaching natural family planning classes with an active baby. Our fourth child was content to remain near us during our two-hour classes, but our fifth child was everywhere. So his sisters, knowing that this baby needed to be near me, took turns coming to class to watch him while we taught. This arrangement worked well for us.

In summary, there seem to be four factors related to non-traumatic separations---the age of the child, the length of the separation, the frequency of separation, and the temporary mother-substitute. My advice to parents is this: Wait until your child is ready. Then by making your initial separations short, you build trust; just about the time he starts to miss you, you're home. Make your separations infrequent; children generally do not like their parents—especially both parents—out of the home several nights a week. Finally choose someone close to your children to be there for them in your absence.

The most common reason given for prolonged breastfeeding is the special relationship that a mother has with her child. This closeness is strengthened over a period of two or three years through the nursing relationship, and this is why the mother is super-sensitive to the needs of her baby and the effect separations have on him.

Natural child spacing involves mother-baby inseparability.

In summary, inseparability is the key to both the duration of ecological breastfeeding and its natural infertility. A mother has to be available to meet her baby's needs. Physical closeness makes the mother more aware of her child's needs—so much so that it is the key requirement for natural spacing and is the basis for the other standards of ecological breastfeeding. For example, frequent and unrestricted nursing—day and night—is a natural consequence of this togetherness. The result is prolonged postpartum infertility and, most importantly, happier mothers and babies.

We have one daughter who is 2½ years old and who is still nursing. She has gone everywhere with us since she's been born and really it has been no problem. In fact, we are so at ease knowing that she is with us and having her needs met by us that the word 'babysitter' is an obsolete word in our household.

* * *

Joshua has been a real joy. He's been to the mountains, the Gulf of Mexico, flown in an airplane, and helped me drive the combine at age six weeks. Truly a portable, happy, easy-to-care-for baby. I'll never go back to cribs and bottles.

1. World Health Organization, "Infant and young child nutrition," Fifty-Fifth World Health Assembly, April 16, 2002.
2. Bonte, M. et al., "Influence of the Socio-Economic Level on the Conception Rate During Lactation," *International Journal of Fertility*, 19 (1974) 97-102.
3. Montessori, Maria. *The Absorbent Mind*, New York: Dell Publishing, 106.
4. Gairdner, William. *War Against the Family*, Toronto: Stoddart Publishing, 1992, 340.
5. Ibid. 338.
6. Thomas, Andrew Peyton. *Crime and the Sacking of America: The Roots of Chaos*, Washington: Brassey's, 1994, 166-7, 170.
7. Campbell, Gerald. "To Heal Spiritual Alienation," Fellowship of Catholic Scholars Convention, September 20, 1997.
8. Such studies are mentioned in my article, *The Crucial First Three Years*, which is available at www.nfpandmore.org.
9. Blakeslee, Sandra. "Studies Show Talking with Infants Shapes Basis of Ability to Think," *The New York Times*, April 17, 1997.
10. *Newsweek* Special Edition, "Your Child From Birth to Three," Spring/Summer 1997.
11. Hotz, Robert Lee. "Study: Babies May Need Hugs to Develop Brain," *The Cincinnati Enquirer*, October 28, 1997.
12. Boyd, Robert. "Scientists Zeroing in on Stress," *The Cincinnati Enquirer*, October 29, 1997.

8

Natural Weaning and the Return of Fertility

"My husband and I are very pleased with this most natural means of spacing children. It is especially great these hectic months after birth when tensions over effectiveness of other methods and adjustments to a new baby can put a strain on a marriage. We feel this way is best for our family in every way and are overjoyed it works so well."

Two opposing but equally false statements about breastfeeding continue to obscure the truth. The first says, "Breastfeeding doesn't space babies." The second says, "You can't get pregnant while breastfeeding." This book and this chapter in particular aim to clarify the realities. First of all, only *ecological* breastfeeding normally provides any significant delay—more than six months--in the return of fertility. Second, even with ecological breastfeeding, most nursing mothers will have their fertility return while still nursing, and most will be able to achieve pregnancy while nursing.

The length of natural child spacing is dependent upon several factors.

With ecological breastfeeding, the return of fertility is related primarily to the frequency and duration of breastfeeding. Eventually the older baby or toddler nurses less and less, and this reduction in breastfeeding normally causes a return of fertility while still nursing. On the other hand, a few mothers will not have a return of menstruation until they are no longer nursing, or a few mothers will have both a return of menstruation and a return of ovulation but will not be able to become pregnant until they are no longer nursing. If a mother has a sick baby who suddenly loses interest in nursing, then she might expect her fertility to return within a few weeks due to the sudden decrease in nursing. Other babies may want to breastfeed exclusively during their illness, and a mother who had already experienced the return of menstruation could go back into amenorrhea due to such constant nursing.

Natural weaning is important for natural child spacing.

Research for years has shown that an early introduction of solids or liquids to the baby causes an early return of fertility to the nursing mother. Likewise pacifier use can bring on an earlier return of fertility to the nursing mother. And any abrupt weaning will initiate the return of fertility.

Natural weaning is not abrupt but very slow and gradual. The weaning process starts as soon as your baby takes anything other than your milk at the breast and ends when your baby or child is no longer breastfeeding. Natural weaning occurs usually over a period of a year or two, sometimes more. The natural weaning that can prolong the child-spacing effect of breastfeeding is a very gradual process that is controlled largely by the baby himself. It is important to remember that most mothers doing eco-breastfeeding will experience more months of postpartum infertility *after* solids are introduced than the duration of infertility they experienced during the first six months of exclusive breastfeeding.

When natural weaning occurs, some babies may wean themselves rather quickly. But most babies will continue to nurse in a frequent and unrestricted manner for a long time even though they have started taking some solid foods. An older baby of increasing size, activity, and appetite may begin to take other food and still continue to nurse as much as before. Since frequent and unrestricted nursing are the major factors in breastfeeding infertility, you can see how gradual, natural weaning can extend postpartum infertility.

When is your baby ready for his first taste of solid food?

The goal for the first six months is easy. Simply enjoy your baby and do exclusive breastfeeding. After that, your baby will probably take to some solid food between six and nine months of life. A few mothers have told me their babies would not accept any other food until one year of age.

Remember that the beginning of solid food does not mean an end to breastfeeding: **solids at first are only a supplement to breastfeeding and not a replacement**. Nursings will continue to be periodic and frequent, if your baby desires them. In order to maintain a good milk supply, it is a good idea to nurse prior to a "solid" feeding, especially during the first stages of introducing other foods.

Continue to offer the breast as needed. Breast milk continues to be a nutritious food for the older baby or toddler and will continue to be his main liquid diet for many more months. Even after he shows an interest in a cup, he will most likely continue to nurse both day and night.

Babies will wean themselves off the breast naturally. With eco-breastfeeding, babies usually wean around their second and third birthdays, and, yes, even their fourth or fifth birthday. The feedings before naps or bedtime are often the last feedings to be dropped.

How long should I nurse?

The American Academy of Pediatrics recommends nursing "for at least the first year of life."[1] On the other hand, the Canadian Paediatric Society recommends breastfeeding for "up to two years and beyond."[2] UNICEF recommends that "breastfeeding should be sustained until the baby is at least two years old."[3] Most medical and breastfeeding organizations encourage mothers to exclusively breastfeed for the first six months of life and to continue breastfeeding. The mother today has many options. She can set her goal for one year or for two years. She can also wait and see how she feels about breastfeeding, a month at a time.

It's sad that many mothers quit nursing during the early months because the experience of nursing an older child becomes even richer and fuller. Mothers have found the practice of baby-led weaning to be very satisfying as indicated by the following stories from three different mothers:

"Our two-year-old weaned himself recently. The first time he quit for a month. Then he resumed for another month and now he has given it up again. I'm glad he did the deciding. It really makes me feel right inside. I know you know the joys of nursing a toddler, but this is the first time for me and it was so rewarding, so special. I do think God was very wise in his plan for babies and mothers."

"My youngest is now four years old and weaned about a week before his fourth birthday. He still has a little try once in a while but informs me I'm empty. I have enjoyed baby-led weaning so much and can see all the advantages so clearly. I only wish I'd been doing this with the first two, although they are reaping the benefits too. I can't think of anything that's more enjoyable and rewarding than being a mother."

"Nursing an older baby seemed to be a particular experience with me as Lennie didn't wean until she was three. Now my arms are so empty. I find much joy in the children as they are growing and maturing, but there is just that special something about breastfeeding that we don't ever experience again."

What are the benefits of breastfeeding?

An extensive study of *developed* countries found that breastfeeding offered definite benefits to both mother and baby. I want to emphasize that here we are looking at mother and baby in First World areas, not in medically or nutritionally deprived areas of the world.

1. Breastfeeding improved the health of the baby by reducing the risk of:
- acute otitis media (ear infections)
- non-specific gastroenteritis
- severe lower respiratory tract infections
- atopic dermatitis
- asthmas in young children
- obesity
- type 1 and type 2 diabetes
- childhood leukemia

- sudden infant death syndrome (SIDS), and
- necrotizing enterocolitis.[4]

2. Breastfeeding improved the health of the mother by reducing her risk of:
- type 2 diabetes
- breast cancer
- ovarian cancer
- postpartum depression[5]

Other studies have shown the benefits for the mother as a result of extended breastfeeding. Here are two examples: one involved rheumatoid arthritis and the other, type 2 diabetes.

1. Those mothers who breastfed for 13 months or more were half as likely to develop rheumatoid arthritis compared to those who had never breastfed.[6]

2. Mothers who breastfed a baby for at least 12 months reduced their risk of getting type 2 diabetes by 15%. If she nursed two babies, each for one year, she had a 30% risk reduction for this disease, and this reduction lasted for 15 years after the birth of her last baby.[7]

The World Health Organization published its study on the *long-term effects* of breastfeeding. The results were attractive:

Subjects who were breastfed experienced lower mean blood pressure and total cholesterol, as well as higher performance in intelligence tests. Prevalence of overweight/obesity and type 2 diabetes was lower among breastfed subjects.[8]

The benefits of breastfeeding are many. This is why the United States government in 2006 began telling mothers that their babies were at risk if they did not breastfed. Considering the benefits of breastfeeding pertaining to the mother, it can also be said that mothers place themselves at increased risk if they do not breastfeed.

The husband's support is important.

With extended breastfeeding the best support a nursing mother can have is her husband. If her husband is 100% behind her decision to breastfeed, then an unkind remark will not hurt nearly as badly. In fact, her husband can step in and handle the discussion, especially when the reaction toward his wife's breastfeeding is strong and negative. In a culture which does not support eco-breastfeeding, it is all the more important for every nursing mother to have loving support from her husband.

Even working mothers can set breastfeeding goals.

Working mothers may choose to exclusively breastfeed for six months. Many working mothers nurse their babies on weekends, all through the night in their bed, before going to work, and after returning from work. These mothers can also pump their milk at work on breaks. Hopefully, working mothers will receive support at their place of employment in their efforts to nurse their babies. Some are lucky and can bring their baby to work and nurse as frequently as their baby desires.

When can I expect menstruation to return if I do eco-breastfeeding?

Two American studies found that menstruation returns, on the average, between 14 and 15 months postpartum for mothers doing eco-breastfeeding.[9,10] In the larger study of the American mothers doing ecological breastfeeding, 70% experienced the return of menstruation between nine and twenty months postpartum, 93% were in amenorrhea at 6 months postpartum, 56% were in amenorrhea at 12 months postpartum, and 33% were still in amenorrhea at 18 months postpartum.[11]

In the United States, a country that discourages mother-baby togetherness, these are good results. Other countries where breastfeeding mothers remain with their babies wherever they go will probably have better results. Of course, there are variations from the average. A few mothers who follow the Seven Standards find their menstrual cycles returning around six months when they were hoping for a longer amenorrhea. On the other hand, a few mothers will go three years or more without any menstruation and this is normal for them. In our survey, but not counted in our studies, we had three breastfeeding mothers who went 41 and 42 months after childbirth without any menstruation. I repeat that this is normal, even if unusual, because the mothers were breastfeeding.

During the natural course of breastfeeding, a mother will eventually experience the return of menstruation. At some point in time the baby will be taking less and less from the breast. The reduced frequency of nursing is probably the major factor in the return of menstruation and fertility even though the baby may still be receiving a good quantity of breast milk. If the weaning is abrupt, the return of menstruation normally occurs several weeks (two to eight) after the nursing has stopped. A few mothers may not menstruate until three months after the breastfeeding has stopped. Any sort of weaning brings with it sooner or later the return of menstruation and fertility.

Extended eco-breastfeeding and extended amenorrhea is normal.

Extended eco-breastfeeding and extended amenorrhea is normal by nature's standards. Taking nature as the norm, the return of menstruation within a few months after childbirth should be the exception for nursing mothers. I say this only in reference to ecological breastfeeding according to the Seven Standards or something very close to it. Ecological breastfeeding with its extended amenorrhea is nature's way of spacing babies.

Some mothers may be concerned when they experience an extended absence of menstruation while breastfeeding. One mother expressed her concern about not having any menstrual cycles when her son was almost three years old:

> I've been told that the length of time it has taken my period to return is not within the "norm." During this time I also tried to get pregnant several times and didn't. I had a thorough checkup with my GYN and everything was fine. I am a breastfeeding peer counselor and no one has come across anyone who has been without menstruation for this long. I thought it would come back as soon as I began working but it didn't. I nurse him mainly throughout the night (he still sleeps with us) and sometimes I nurse a couple of times during the day.
>
> I began to worry because lactation consultants and breastfeeding peer counselors were taken aback by the length of time I have been without a period. I would get weird looks from everyone including nurses and the doctor. I was asked if I was pregnant and are you sure you're not pregnant. Or,

"Did you check with the doctor?" Or, "Are you sure nothing is wrong?" Or I was told to "Get an exam for your thyroid." This is why I was so concerned. Funny looks and questions like these will make anyone who is not familiar with this situation a bit concerned.

This mother appreciated my telling her that her situation was perfectly normal. She contacted me later to say her periods returned two days after her child turned three years old.

I hope that in the future medical and nursing schools will teach eco-breastfeeding so that breastfeeding mothers will not have to endure the questions and remarks that this mother received. Medical schools should be teaching that the normal return of fertility with ecological breastfeeding can be described in standard statistical terms. For example, the previously mentioned 70% of returns between 9 and 20 months is almost a classic example of the range within what statisticians call the first standard deviation in a normal distribution. The return of fertility at 36 months is probably at the far end of the third standard duration. When this becomes common knowledge, the informed mom might quip, "Well, being in the third standard deviation isn't average, but it's still part of a normal distribution."

What if I have early postpartum bleeding or spotting?

Here we have to distinguish between "exclusive breastfeeding" and "ecological breastfeeding."

1. If you are doing *exclusive* breastfeeding, studies show that you can ignore any vaginal bleeding as a sign of fertility during the first eight weeks after childbirth.[12] After eight weeks, you have over a 98% natural infertility rate with exclusive breastfeeding until your baby reaches six months of age provided that you are still experiencing breastfeeding amenorrhea, that is, no periods.[13] Once you have a true period or once you complete six months of exclusive breastfeeding, you should assume that fertility has returned or is just around the corner unless you are eco-breastfeeding.

If you experience spotting or a day or so of bleeding between eight weeks and six months when doing exclusive breastfeeding, I don't know your fertility status. The conservative approach would be to assume you are fertile or will be very soon and to start the standard observations and periodic abstinence of systematic natural family planning or simply look forward to pregnancy. I would also suggest that you switch to the full practice of the Seven Standards of eco-breastfeeding.

2. If you are nursing according to the *Seven Standards* and experience spotting or bleeding in the early months, be aware that some mothers have increased their nursings and have remained in amenorrhea. On the other hand, spotting may be a warning that menstruation or ovulation is around the corner. A few mothers have conceived after spotting and without having had a regular menstruation. If a mother experiences pre-menstrual feelings or spotting during these early months, she might re-evaluate her schedule and aim for more rest and nursing. With our fifth baby, I had pre-menstrual feelings and made a special effort to rest more at naptime and also during the night and to let the baby nurse often during those rest times. The pre-menstrual feelings left and there was no menstruation. If a mother experiences such spotting or bleeding and is concerned about the return of fertility, she can begin charting for signs of possible fertility.

The return of menstruation is usually associated with the return of fertility.

The return of menstruation is generally a strong indicator of the return of fertility. Many nursing mothers have relied successfully on breastfeeding infertility during amenorrhea. Some breastfeeding mothers experience one to three infertile cycles after the return of menstruation. A few nursing mothers will have many infertile cycles and will have to wait longer to achieve a pregnancy. Some nursing mothers will ovulate prior to the return of menstruation. As research shows later in this chapter, about 6% of nursing mothers who have babies six months or older will become pregnant before their first period, assuming regular intercourse and no fertility awareness or periodic abstinence. If mothers want additional spacing beyond what breastfeeding gives them, they can learn their fertility signs and practice systematic natural family planning.[14]

A few mothers will not be able to get pregnant while breastfeeding. One friend charted perfect fertility cycles while breastfeeding her first baby, but she was not able to achieve pregnancy. A doctor well informed about breastfeeding and natural infertility saw her charts and told her she would become pregnant the first cycle after weaning. Her baby weaned when two years old and she promptly proved the doctor right. This mother, however, went on to prove that history does not necessarily repeat itself, and she became pregnant while nursing her second baby.

If a breastfeeding mother desires another pregnancy, she may find that she will have to be patient and wait on nature. This is particularly hard for older mothers who desire more children. A good knowledge of the fertility signs may be of help in achieving pregnancy sooner.

The return of fertility does not mean an end to nursing. A mother can continue to nurse her baby or child while having menstrual cycles and even while pregnant.

Weaning may occur during pregnancy because of the baby's reaction or because of the mother's reaction. The mother may react negatively to nursing due to hormonal changes even though she had planned to nurse throughout the pregnancy. She may suddenly find nursing very painful. In this situation the older child will usually accept back rubs or other alternatives when he realizes how painful the nursing is to his mother. Other children may wean because the milk tastes different or is reduced in quantity.

Some mothers continue to satisfy the child's needs at the breast while pregnant and continue to nurse both the baby and other child after childbirth. Nursing two siblings is called tandem nursing and has been done for centuries. This is especially true in other cultures where prolonged lactation is common.

What is the baby-spacing effectiveness of ecological breastfeeding while in amenorrhea?

Eco-breastfeeding is highly effective during the first six months postpartum. During the first three months of ecological breastfeeding and lactation amenorrhea, the probability of becoming pregnant is almost nil. During the next three months of amenorrhea and ecological breastfeeding, the chance of pregnancy is at the one percent level. The earliest return of fertility I've seen recorded by someone doing ecological breastfeeding was at four and one-half months, based on her mucus and temperature record and followed by her first period. She always experienced an early return of fertility while breastfeeding. Her older relatives had the same experience. She took natural family planning classes and found the information to be very helpful. She had ample warning with the mucus and a good temperature shift prior to the return of her first menstruation. With abstinence according to the rules taught to this couple, they were able to avoid pregnancy and she continued to nurse their baby.

After six months postpartum, the chance of becoming pregnant while experiencing breastfeeding amenorrhea without any abstinence or fertility awareness is 6%. In these cases ovulation occurs prior to what would have been the first menstrual period if pregnancy had not occurred. That figure is based on several studies. In 1897, Remfry found a 5% pregnancy rate before the first period among breastfeeding mothers.[15] In 1969 Bonte and van Balem found a similar rate of 5.4% in Rwanda.[16] In 1971 Prem reported a rate of 5-6% among American breastfeeding mothers.[17]

Charting your fertility signs may prove invaluable.

For mothers who do not desire another pregnancy at this time and are concerned about the risk of pregnancy prior to the return of menstruation, proper instruction in systematic natural family planning can reduce that risk to close to one percent.[18] Even for mothers desiring immediate pregnancy, I would still encourage natural family planning charting because the upward shift in temperatures right after ovulation is the best indicator of your baby's age during pregnancy. This evidence may save you unnecessary tests and expense; it may prevent also a premature induced delivery. Based on your chart your due date may be later than your doctor's due date which is based on the start of your last menstrual period or other indicators. Your charted daily temperature readings are truly scientific and very helpful data. The temperature graph is the single most accurate method of estimating the date of conception and therefore gestational age, according to Dr. Konald Prem, professor emeritus of the Department of Obstetrics and Gynecology of the University of

Minnesota School of Medicine—even more accurate than ultrasound.[19] The charting information is always helpful in estimating the date of childbirth, and it's even more important in high-risk pregnancies or complications or when the pregnancy occurs before the first postpartum menses. For the doctor who is concerned because he thinks you are overdue, the chart can either confirm his opinion or show otherwise.

One couple demonstrated the conception date of their baby using their sympto-thermal chart and Dr. Prem's article above on gestational age and the temperature sign. This information convinced their insurance company that their baby was conceived after her husband had started his new job, and the company agreed to pay the costs involved with their baby's premature birth.

To determine the due date, you take the first day of elevated temperatures associated with ovulation, subtract 7 days, and then add 9 months. This determination can be used for a pregnancy achieved during amenorrhea, during a long cycle, or in a normal cycle of the breastfeeding mother.

Extended amenorrhea does not impair fertility.

The general experience of those mothers with long durations of lactation amenorrhea is that normal fertility is not impaired once menstruation returns or once the child is completely weaned. One of the mothers who experienced over 40 months of breastfeeding amenorrhea was most appreciative of the information found in the first edition of *Breastfeeding and Natural Child Spacing*: "I could have wasted money and time in doctors' offices thinking I was abnormal." She found that once her cycles returned, they were regular and ovulation occurred each month. Many mothers also experience another pregnancy shortly after breastfeeding amenorrhea ends, showing that fertility has not been impaired by the breastfeeding experience.

Eco-breastfeeding does space babies.

Couples starting their families may use eco-breastfeeding alone to space their children's births. We call this Plan A. In my opinion, it's the preferred plan for spacing babies. With proper knowledge and support and the practice of ecological breastfeeding, the average nursing mother will experience an extended duration of infertility recognizable by the long absence of menstruation. If no form of conception regulation is used except ecological breastfeeding, babies on the average will be born about two years apart.

> I appreciated your encouragement to continue following child-led weaning. I had a period a couple of days after writing to you. It was the first one following 26 months of amenorrhea. I was ecstatic, almost as excited as I was at age 14 when I had my first menstrual period! I began charting immediately, ovulated and conceived. I did wean our son during my pregnancy, but at a pace that suited us both.

* * *

> The other day someone was complaining of cramps and discomfort with her period, and I mentioned that since my first baby I have never had all that cramping and pain with my periods. Then I said: "But come to think of it, I've had so few periods." And my friend said, "You know, you are the truly liberated woman!" How true! So far I have had 11 periods in over eight years. That is with three babies. Our 15 month old is nursing three or four times a day and I haven't had a period yet.

1. American Academy of Pediatrics, "Policy Statement: Breastfeeding and the Use of Human Milk," Pediatrics, February 2005.
2. Canadian Paediatric Society, News Release: "Extend exclusive breastfeeding to six months, advise paediatricians," March 8, 2005.
3. UNICEF, Breastfeeding: Foundation for a Healthy Future, August 1999.
4. Ip, S. et al, "Breastfeeding and Maternal and Infant Health Outcomes in Developed Countries," Agency for Healthcare Research and Quality, April 2007.
5. Ibid.
6. Pikwer M., et al (2008) "Breastfeeding, but not oral contraceptives, is associated with a reduced risk of rheumatoid arthritis, *Annals of the Rheumatic Diseases*, doi:10.1136/ard.2007.084707. Online May 13, 2008.
7. Stuebe, A., et al. "Duration of Lactation and Incidence of Type 2 Diabetes," *Journal of the American Medical Association*, 94 (Nov. 23/30, 2005) 2601-2610.
8. Horta, B. L. et al, "Evidence on the long-term effects of breastfeeding," WHO, 2007.

9. Kippley, S. and J. "The Relation Between Breastfeeding and Amenorrhea: Report of a Survey," *JOGN Nursing*, November-December 1972, 15-21. Available at www.nfpandmore.org.

10. Kippley, S. and J. "The Spacing of Babies with Ecological Breastfeeding," *International Review*, Spring-Summer 1989, 107-116. Available at www.nfpandmore.org.

11. Kippley, 1989.

12. "Consensus Statement: Breastfeeding as a Family Planning Method," *Lancet*, November 19, 1988, 1204-5.

13. Ibid.

14. A free natural family planning manual is available at www.nfpandmore.org.

15. Remfry, L. "The Effects of Lactation on Menstruation and Pregnation," *Transactions of the Obstetrical Society of London*, 38(1897), 22-27. Available at www.nfpandmore.org.

16. Bonte, M. and van Balem, H. "Prolonged Lactation and Family Spacing in Rwanda," *Journal of Biosocial Science*, April 1969, 97-100.

17. Prem, Konald. "Post-Partum Ovulation," Unpublished paper presented at the La Leche League International Conference, Chicago, July 1971. Available at www.nfpandmore.org.

18. See free NFP manual at www.nfpandmore.org.

19. Prem, K. "Assessment of Gestational Age," *Minnesota Medicine*, September 1976, 623. Available at www.nfpandmore.org.

9

Natural Child Spacing

"Throughout the world as a whole, more births are prevented by lactation than all other forms of contraception put together."
—Dr. R.V. Short, Scotland 1976[1]

"Breastfeeding offered more protection than all methods of contraception combined." —Dr. Peter Howie, United Kingdom, 1986[2]

All Seven Standards are important. Almost all mothers have the ability to breastfeed their babies, take care of them naturally, and experience breastfeeding's natural effect of extended infertility. There is, however, a huge difference between being capable of something and actually doing it. In order for a mother to space the births of her babies naturally through breastfeeding, she needs to follow the natural baby care program of the Seven Standards, or, in other words, she needs to do ecological breastfeeding. Natural baby care and natural child spacing go hand-in-hand. Whether or not a mother experiences breastfeeding's natural child spacing depends mostly on how she chooses to breastfeed and care for her baby.

All choices involving the Seven Standards are important. Is she going to exclusively breastfeed for the first six months postpartum? Is she going to care for her baby at the breast naturally, or is she going to nurse but also offer breast substitutes? Is she going to sleep with her baby during the night? Will she take a daily nap with her nursing baby? Will she allow her baby to use the breast for non-nutritive suckling? Will she be one with her baby? Will she take her baby with her on errands and trips? Is she going to follow the complete ecological breastfeeding program? Ecological breastfeeding calls for a beautiful oneness of mother and baby, a biological oneness that is important and crucial if the mother wants natural child spacing. The Seven Standards more or less guarantee that biological unity.

How parenting choices impact fertility

An example of how parenting can influence the return of fertility is seen in the following case. With her first two babies this mother used only breastfeeding to space her babies. With her first baby she exclusively breastfed for the first five months and stopped nursing when her baby was 11 months old. She gave night feedings for the first eight months and offered a pacifier frequently. Her menstruation returned at six months postpartum and conception occurred at 12 months postpartum.

With her second baby the mother nursed and slept with her baby for 26 months. Solids were offered at six months, but the baby did not take them until seven or eight months of age. This baby never had a pacifier. Menstruation returned at 24 months postpartum and conception occurred at 25 months postpartum. As we see here, her mothering practices changed with her second baby and gave her two years of amenorrhea while a more cultural form of breastfeeding with her first baby gave her only 6 months of amenorrhea. Her mothering practices with her second baby followed the pattern of ecological breastfeeding, and that is why she went two years after childbirth without any menstrual periods.

For most mothers the natural spacing mechanism is a very delicate one. Eliminating just one of the Seven Standards may shorten or eliminate any natural spacing effect for a particular woman. Most mothers need lots of frequent and unrestricted nursing to hold back menstruation. Thus is why it is important for mothers to follow all Seven Standards if they desire natural spacing.

Population and the importance of breastfeeding

More attention should be given to the role that ecological breastfeeding can play in the birthrates not just of individual couples but also entire cultures. The presence of breastfeeding is a key factor in the low birthrates of some cultures, and the decline in breastfeeding is an important factor in increased birthrates in others.

Doctor Otto Schaefer studied the relationship between shortened lactation and the population increase among the Canadian Eskimos who previously had small families through prolonged lactation of about three years. In fact, he found that the traditional completed family size was three to four children through traditional breastfeeding alone.[3]

Doctors J. A. Hildes and Otto Schaefer conducted some fascinating studies on the Igloolik Eskimos. Their one outstanding observation dealt with the difference in the fertility rates among the older women as contrasted with the younger women due to changes in mothering practices. Women aged 30 to 50 years who had traditionally breastfed conceived 20 to 30 months after childbirth. Remember, that is when they conceived, not when they gave birth. The younger mothers under 30 years of age who used the baby bottle conceived 2 to 4 months after childbirth. The doctors found the rapid urbanization of these Eskimos during the twenty post-World War II years was responsible for the increase in births. Urbanization brought the baby bottle to this people, and they lost the natural birth spacing that prolonged breastfeeding had previously given them.[4] The population explosion experienced by the Canadian Eskimos was recorded by Schaefer to be a 60% increase in the mid-1950s, due to "the increasing use of bottle-feeding and the shortening of lactation."[5]

At the Fourth National and International Symposium on Natural Family Planning, Dr. Peter Howie of the United Kingdom added an interesting research statistic. In 1976, a calculation was made about developing countries in the non-Communist world where about 85% of rural and 75% of urban women breastfed; it was determined that breastfeeding offered 4 to 8 months of additional infertility or provided 31½ million couple-years of infertility. That is, "31½ million couples would not have a conception because of breastfeeding in a single year." That means that breastfeeding provided more pregnancy avoidance than all the unnatural forms of birth control (condoms, IUDs, pills, etc.) put together which was estimated at 24 million couple-years of fertility protection at that time. Howie is convinced that the world population has increased significantly during the last 1,000 years because of artificial baby milk and baby food.[6] He concluded his talk:

> I have tried to give you some insight into the importance of breastfeeding as a means of spacing families. Breastfeeding is the naturally evolved method of controlling fertility. Studies of traditional communities show that humans were not intended to have huge, uncontrolled fertility which is observed among the urban poor of the developing world. By discarding lactation, modern man has created the problems associated with hyper-fertility, which creates havoc with both maternal and child health. By preserving breastfeeding in the developing world and rediscovering it in the developed world, we can take an important step towards restoring family spacing to its intended and natural state.[7]

Personal Research

To test the theory that ecological breastfeeding spaces babies for American women just as it does for women in primitive and developing parts of the world, my husband and I conducted two studies, one in 1971 and another in 1986. In both studies the readers of the early editions of *Breastfeeding and Natural Child Spacing* returned a survey about their recent breastfeeding experiences. In both studies we used the first postpartum menstruation or any form of spotting as an indication of the end of amenorrhea and the return of fertility. We realize that this is not the best determination of fertility; the temperature graph is far superior. Nevertheless, any spotting or bleeding provides a very conservative indication of the end of amenorrhea.

What we found in both studies confirmed our basic conviction that ecological breastfeeding provides significantly more postpartum infertility than cultural breastfeeding. The results showed that on the average babies will be spaced about two years apart with ecological breastfeeding, assuming random intercourse and no form of birth control and no use of systematic periodic abstinence. The larger study in 1986 will be reviewed below.

The 1986 study

During a 15-year period we accumulated over 1500 breastfeeding surveys. A data analysis computer program was developed, and a student nurse entered 286 surveys for analysis. We stopped inputting when periodic analysis showed that further surveys would not change the results. The surveys in the study were not pre-selected, but we did omit those surveys with an exceptionally long amenorrhea. Using the same six criteria we used in 1971, we found 98 nursing experiences that qualified as ecological breastfeeding.[8]

1. No pacifiers used
2. No bottles used
3. No liquids or solids for five months
4. No feeding schedules other than baby's
5. Presence of night feedings
6. Presence of lying-down nursing for naps and night feedings.

Total months of breastfeeding

One of the biggest differences between the two surveys was the average duration of breastfeeding for the entire sample. In the 1986 study, the 286 breastfeeding experiences averaged 20.4 months, 25% longer than the 16.3 average duration in the 1971 survey. We speculated that this increase may be due to two facts: 1) an increased social acceptance of more extended breastfeeding and 2) reading *Breastfeeding and Natural Child Spacing* may have motivated mothers to nurse longer.

Duration of amenorrhea

The average duration of amenorrhea for the 286 nursing experiences was 11.7 months compared with 10.2 in 1971. The sample of 98 eco-breastfeeding experiences averaged 14.5 months of amenorrhea. We think this was the most important finding of this study because it confirmed the primary finding of the 1971 study where we found an average of 14.6 months of breastfeeding amenorrhea with ecological breastfeeding. We now have two studies 15 years apart yielding almost identical results on this key point, so we can say with even greater confidence than before that American women or women elsewhere in a bottle-feeding culture who follow the pattern of ecological breastfeeding will average 14.5 months of amenorrhea.

Comparison between ecological and cultural breastfeeding

We also compared the eco-breastfeeding group with the cultural breastfeeding group, and the results are illustrated in Table 1. That is, we separated the 286 surveys into two separate groups, something we failed to do in the 1971 study. For some reason, two surveys failed to be tallied, so the total is 284.

Table 1
Comparison of Duration of Amenorrhea

Ecological Breastfeeding
    N = 98
        Average Months of Breastfeeding: 25.7
        Average Months of Amenorrhea: 14.5

Cultural Breastfeeding
    N = 186
        Average Months of Breastfeeding: 17.5
        Average Months of Amenorrhea: 10.3

The ecological breastfeeding mothers averaged approximately 40% greater duration of amenorrhea than the cultural breastfeeding mothers.

We then tried to discover if there was any single one of the six criteria we used for ecological breastfeeding that by itself showed an even greater duration of amenorrhea, but we found none. Since we were unable to find any single factor which could be effective for 12 months or more, we were confirmed in our conviction that it is a combination of all the elements of ecological breastfeeding that yields the side effect of a year or more of natural infertility, on the average. Our research therefore confirms that it is the entire package of ecological breastfeeding that spaces babies.

Variation and possible causes

Significant variation in the return of menstruation continued to be recorded among mothers doing ecological breastfeeding. Of these cases, 93% were in amenorrhea at six months, 56% were still in amenorrhea at one year, and 34% were still in amenorrhea at 18 months.

We do not know what causes this sort of variation. If two mothers follow the eco-breastfeeding program, why does one have a return of menstruation at six months and the other at 16 or 26 months? Undoubtedly some of the variation in the length of amenorrhea can be attributed to the differences in the suckling needs and nursing patterns of different babies. In addition there are probably differences in the way bodies of different women respond to the same amount of suckling stimulus.

Perhaps the best explanation is that the return of fertility with eco-breastfeeding has a statistically normal distribution, with a range of 9 to 20 months in about the first standard deviation and extremely early or delayed returns in the third standard deviation. This explanation would take into account differences in both mothers' and babies' bodies and in individual nursing patterns that were still within the definition of ecological breastfeeding.

All past and current research dealing with breastfeeding infertility supports the basic thesis of this book: ecological breastfeeding with its frequent and unrestricted suckling of the baby at the breast is nature's way of spacing babies.

Natural child spacing

Women can't practice breastfeeding or use natural child spacing if they don't have babies. Most industrialized Western countries have a negative birth rate, and an increasing number of these countries are encouraging mothers to have babies. More churches should do what they can to encourage couples to have children. In my country you see a decline in the number of children at our churches and schools are closing. On the other hand, in 2006 the fertility rate hit 2.1 in the United States, the highest level since 1971 and enough for a generation to replace itself.[9] I believe if more mothers breastfed, they might have an increased desire to have another baby. I certainly don't want people to say that I am promoting small families in my promotion of extended natural breastfeeding infertility. On the contrary, I see a need for more couples to choose to have children and to be generous in having children.

On the other hand, I am also aware for years that mothers who have a baby each year can become overwhelmed. While editing this book I received a phone call from a friend who told me that some mothers in her area were having surprise pregnancies resulting in large families, as in double digits, with close birth intervals. Several of these mothers experienced emotional problems and sought counseling. These mothers were not using the cross-checking method we teach for systematic natural family planning, nor did they do ecological breastfeeding.

The point here is that nature meant for mothers to have a rest after childbirth, but most modern societies encourage mothers to do the kind of baby care that is not conducive to natural child spacing. Unfortunately, many natural family planning teachers do not instruct couples in all the known fertility signs nor do they teach the Seven Standards of ecological breastfeeding.

Ecological breastfeeding isn't going to cure all the world's problems, even in our personal families. But in this book, I have tried to show its far reaching effects in our families and in the world at large. At the level of both the individual family and the world, it provides a natural form of birth regulation as well as significant and prolonged health benefits. It would seem more than appropriate that ecological breastfeeding would be encouraged at all levels.

My dream is that the Seven Standards will become common knowledge among all those who influence parents—doctors, nurses, teachers, pastors, NFP teachers, and social workers—as well as among the general laity. The U. S. federal government has finally gotten the word and is telling moms that they are placing their babies "at risk" if they do not breastfeed. It's high time the rest of the world's opinion shapers get on board.

Professionals do change. I consider Dr. Otto Schaefer to be one of the leading pioneers for the promotion of breastfeeding and natural child spacing. Yet, as a German doctor working among the Inuit in the Arctic, he first taught the "merits" of formula feeding. He was constantly writing down in his notebook everything he observed about his patients and soon realized he was wrong about formula. The good doctor later taught that "breastfeeding had a greater influence on the life and health of infants than any other single factor," and that "the traditional Inuit custom of breastfeeding up until the age of three years… provided an effective type of birth control. The natural contraceptive action of lactation allowed for a desirable spacing of children."[10] We need more professionals like him.

Healthy birth intervals

What is the best interval to have between births? The Centers for Disease Control and Prevention studied 173,205 births in Utah from 1989 to 1996. The study found that babies were at higher risk for poor health if mothers had their babies too soon or too far apart. The study concluded that the best spacing was a 2½ year interval.[11] One study of a selected culture is more suggestive than conclusive, and what it suggests is that the natural spacing of 24 to 30 months enjoyed by most parents doing ecological breastfeeding is truly in tune with nature. As some experts have stressed, "Nature knows best."

Economically, the couple's overall health costs should be lower for both mother and baby in the years to come. The couple may choose to homeschool. If so, it will be easier to have the children spaced for such schooling, and a little distance in age is a benefit when one older sibling helps a younger sibling with his learning and work. If the couple choose to send their children to parochial or private schools, it is easier to handle the tuitions when the children are spaced about two to three years apart.

Likewise, parents benefit from the experience of raising the first child and this experience helps them to parent better when the second child is born. The spacing gives the mother the additional time to meet the present baby's needs, and the extra time helps the mother emotionally. As one friend told me, "I do not want to have three babies in diapers." Even with help from family and friends, such situations can be exhausting.

Couples learn patience when they cannot get pregnant while nursing their two year old. They learn acceptance when their periods return at nine months postpartum instead of the 19 months they had hoped for. If the couple has an early return of menstruation and also has a serious reason to postpone pregnancy, then the couple can begin charting the fertility signs to determine the return of fertility and practice systematic NFP to further postpone pregnancy.[12]

NFP is green

Eco-breastfeeding is "green." Ecological breastfeeding does not pollute in any way. There is no industrial production of milk or milk bottles or pacifiers or breast pumps. Nothing is discarded in the air, the ground, or the waters. The production and disposal of sanitary pads is greatly reduced. Wouldn't it be great if all the environmentalists promoted the Seven Standards and systematic natural family planning as well.

The sex-hormone residues of the birth control pill have contaminated the waters of twenty-four metropolitan cities.[13] The solution for this problem is natural family planning whether it be systematic NFP or ecological breastfeeding. Neither pollutes the environment.

Ecological breastfeeding is a wonderful way for parents to plan their families naturally. Most couples who choose this option will be grateful for this benefit and the many other benefits associated with extended breastfeeding. Nature's way of spacing babies should be more widely promoted.

Not just for Catholics

Unfortunately some assume that natural child spacing is just a Catholic issue. Not so. What this book teaches is basically how the female body works after childbirth. As a teenager I first learned about this aspect of the female body in a high school physiology class when an older teacher mentioned that the reproductive cycle does not end at childbirth; it ends with breastfeeding. At that time I really didn't understand what she meant. But I was reminded of her teaching years later when I gained the knowledge in my search for the truth. The physiology of the female body should be of interest to those of all religious beliefs and to the non-religious as well.

To show the appreciation of women from various faiths, I conclude this chapter with some of their quotes.

Our daughter is 4½. We used the method for over two years before we conceived her, so it's definitely worked well for us. We are not Catholic.

* * *

You may also wonder if I am of a faith that does not condone birth control means. No, I am not, and I have in fact taken the pill for a year and a half between my two children. My boys are over three years apart, as I remained sterile for nearly a year after those pills. So I've found breastfeeding a lovely blessing in every way, and the infertility is only a convenient side effect. We've decided on a third child at the earliest possible date—considering the breastfeeding situation, of course.

* * *

As a Protestant, ecological breastfeeding had never been presented to my husband and me as a logical way to have a family. Our sweet little one is nine days old, and she will be the first one not to have a pacifier. Many of my acquaintances are put right on the IUD after their first baby, and I think it's a shame when God intended His way of spacing little ones.

* * *

My religion, Islam, encourages breastfeeding for two years and, according to some Muslim scholars, allows birth control to be practiced within that two-year period. I feel that so many people ignore breastfeeding as a form of natural child spacing. The techniques you describe are entirely compatible with my religion.

* * *

My daughter is 13 months old and we're enjoying the breastfeeding relationship. I like the amenorrhea, and my husband and I are pleased with the absence of artificial birth control. I am enjoying full-time mothering following four years as a social worker. My husband is a new family practice physician. He promotes breastfeeding at every opportunity and out of personal conviction does not prescribe the Pill or fit IUDs for patients.

* * *

My husband is a pastor so we have many outside obligations to fulfill. We take our seven-month-old baby everywhere and when she is hungry or needs pacifying, I am there with her. Regarding breastfeeding, I was amazingly alone in my decisions to do this. Even so-called "progressive" mothers rely on formula and/or pacifiers. But I have found great support in women of my grandmother's age.

---

1. Short, R. "The Evolution of Human Reproduction," *Proc. R. Soc. Lond.*, 195 (1976) 3-24.
2. Howie, P. " Synopsis of Research on Breastfeeding and Fertility," *Breastfeeding and Natural Family Planning*, Bethesda, Maryland: KM Associates, 1986, 7-22.
3. Hankins, Gerald. *Sunrise Over Pangnirtung: The Story of Otto Schaefer, M.D.*, Calgary, Alberta: The Arctic Institute of North America of the University of Calgary, 2000, 192.
4. Hildes, J. and Schaefer, O. "Health of Igloolik Eskimos and Changes with Urbanization." Paper presented at the Circumpolar Health Symposium, Oulu, Finland, June 1971.
5. Schaefer, Otto. "When the Eskimo Comes to Town," *Nutrition Today*, November/December 1971.
6. Howie, P. "Synopsis of Research on Breastfeeding and Fertility," *Breastfeeding and Natural Family Planning*, Bethesda, Maryland: KM Associates, 1986, 7-22.
7. Ibid.
8. Kippley, S. and J. "The Spacing of Babies with Ecological Breastfeeding," *International Review*, Spring/Summer 1989, 107-116.
9. "Fertility rate in U. S. highest since 1971," *The Cincinnati Enquirer*, December 20, 2007, A5.
10. Hankins, 180. His book on the life of Dr. Otto Schaefer, *Sunrise Over Pangnirtung* is fascinating.
11. Zhu, B. et al, "Effect of the interval between pregnancies on perinatal outcomes," *New England Journal of Medicine* 340 (1999) 589-94.
12. Free natural family planning instruction is available by downloading the NFP manual at www.nfpandmore.org.
13. Mendoza, Martha. "Showdown set on drugs in water," *The Cincinnati Enquirer*, April 14, 2008, A3.

10

Natural Family Planning

"Our results show that 0.4 unintended pregnancies occurred per 100 women years, if there was abstinence during the fertile time." —a German study, 2007[1]

There are two forms of natural family planning: 1) ecological breastfeeding according to the Seven Standards and 2) systematic natural family planning (NFP). We sometimes refer to them as Plan A and Plan B. With Plan A, couples use only ecological breastfeeding to space their babies. However, sometimes a couple needs additional spacing when fertility returns, and they turn to a form of systematic NFP or Plan B.

Most of this book is devoted to eco-breastfeeding, but it's important to give at least a brief introduction to systematic NFP. There are different forms of systematic NFP, but the essence of all of them is the same: chaste abstinence during the fertile time for the avoidance of pregnancy. The oldest form of NFP was calendar rhythm, sometimes called the rhythm method, a system that estimated the fertile time in the current cycle solely on the basis of previous cycle history. It could be used very effectively by couples if the wife had fairly regular cycles and the spouses knew and followed the rules. However, because of various kinds of cycle irregularities and poor teaching, it was ineffective for many couples, and almost no one teaches that form of NFP today.

Contemporary forms of systematic NFP focus on a woman's ongoing fertility signs that can be observed and recorded on a daily basis. The common signs of fertility are the secretion of cervical mucus, some physical changes that occur in the cervix, and changes that occur in a woman's waking temperature. Some forms of systematic NFP focus almost exclusively on the appearance and disappearance of cervical mucus. Other forms of systematic NFP focus on cervical mucus but also use the temperature and cervix signs, frequently in a way that crosschecks the mucus sign. Systems that focus almost exclusively on the mucus sign are generally described as the "Ovulation Method," a term first invented by Dr. John Billings of Australia. Systems that use the signs in a cross-checking way are called variations of the Sympto-Thermal Method (STM) or simply a Cross-Check Method.

Our preference is to teach couples how to use all the common signs of fertility and infertility. Couples can then use the signs in a cross-checking way, or they can use only one sign, such as a mucus-only or a temperature-only system. The choice is theirs, but in order to make an informed choice, they have to know the options. If you investigate this widely, you will probably find some who will say that learning more than one sign causes confusion. Some might also infer that the more you pay for an NFP course, the better it must be. We respectfully disagree on both points.

A recent study of the Sympto-Thermal Method

The lead author of the study quoted at the top of this chapter, Dr. Petra Frank-Herrmann of the natural family planning section of the Department of Gynecological Endocrinology at the University of Heidelberg, commented on the results in early 2007.

"For a contraceptive method to be rated as highly efficient as the hormonal pill, there should be less than one pregnancy per 100 women per year when the method is used correctly. The pregnancy rate for women who used the Sympto-Thermal Method (STM) correctly in our study was 0.4%, which can be interpreted as one pregnancy occurring per 250 women per year. Therefore, we maintain that the effectiveness of the STM is comparable to the effectiveness of modern methods such as oral contraceptives, and is an effective and acceptable method of family planning."[2]

The professor in this German study also emphasized that the Sympto-Thermal Method can be learned through a book or a class. After all, the STM is not rocket science. My husband and I believe that most couples can learn the cross-checking STM well by using the book, *Natural Family Planning*, at our website, www.nfpandmore.org. This easy-to-understand "How-to" manual teaches both the STM and ecological breastfeeding and can be downloaded without cost.

The breastfeeding mother

Of particular importance for the nursing mother in determining the return of fertility is the observation of cervical mucus and the cervix. As we noted in an earlier chapter, the available evidence indicates that about 6% of mothers doing eco-breastfeeding with babies six months or older will experience pregnancy before menstruation returns, assuming random intercourse and no fertility awareness and related abstinence. To find out if she is in that small group for whom fertility comes before her first menstruation, the nursing mother who needs to postpone pregnancy further can observe and chart her signs of fertility or infertility. Most breastfeeding mothers who have learned their fertility signs will notice an abundance of cervical mucus prior to their first ovulation or prior to their first menstrual cycle.

The temperature sign is also extremely helpful when breastfeeding. It assures the mother that she is not pregnant. It also is a good predictor of the return of fertility.

The well-informed nursing mother can almost always detect the onset of fertility before her first postpartum menstruation. For example, a friend who spoke at a New York conference on natural child spacing told her audience that she had been in breastfeeding amenorrhea for a long time but realized from her observations that she had ovulated recently and would start her period during the conference. She brought along the necessary equipment, and she did indeed start her first postpartum period at the conference. The mothers in attendance were simply amazed that she knew ahead of time that this would happen.

Furthermore, a mother can nurse as long as she desires and still practice natural family planning successfully. This is important. A nursing mother does not have to wean in order to practice any form of systematic NFP, especially the STM.

The STM is easy to learn, easy to use, inexpensive, and healthy. It involves current history. The bottom line is this: there are three commonly recognized signs of fertility and infertility: mucus, temperature, and cervix. You can learn to observe these and use them in a cross-checking way. This information is helpful in avoiding or achieving pregnancy. It can be used effectively in normal or irregular cycles, and you can use it to monitor the return of fertility while breastfeeding.

Seeking pregnancy while breastfeeding

Couples desiring pregnancy once fertility has returned should chart daily waking temperatures as well as the mucus signs. The temperature shift is the best indicator of the unborn baby's age and can be extremely helpful if any concerns develop later. Oftentimes with nursing, ovulation and the temperature shift may occur one or two weeks later than usual. If this happens and conception occurs, your true "due date" would be one or two weeks later than an estimate based on your last menstrual period. If you become pregnant before your first postpartum menstruation, the upward temperature shift is all the more valuable as a marker of gestational age. In addition, the temperature sign gives you an early confirmation of pregnancy. With three weeks of elevated temperatures, you have a 99% certainty that you are pregnant. On the other hand, a constant low temperature pattern tells a nursing mother that she is not pregnant. The knowledge attained by systematic natural family planning can be very practical.

If a couple is having difficulty achieving pregnancy, they should definitely read Marilyn Shannon's book, *Fertility, Cycles and Nutrition*.[3] This book is helpful for infertility as well as PMS, painful periods, premenopause, repeated miscarriages, irregular cycles, heavy bleeding and even male infertility. As one doctor said, "This book is the best self-help book for women." For example, improved nutrition can help to lengthen the luteal phase (the post-ovulation part of the cycle) and to improve thyroid functioning, thus helping women to achieve pregnancy. This book is invaluable for a couple seeking pregnancy or for women having problems with their fertility-menstrual cycles.

NFP International

Never before in human history has it been so easy for so many couples to learn their times of cyclic fertility and infertility and to learn natural child spacing through breastfeeding. NFP International was founded primarily for the purpose of teaching the Seven Standards of ecological breastfeeding, the cross-checking sympto-thermal method, and the covenant theology of human sexuality. A free NFP manual and many resources in support of natural family planning and related issues are at the NFP International website, www.nfpandmore.org.

Support for breastfeeding

We mentioned that a couple can get support for systematic NFP at the NFP International website as well as lots of information about ecological breastfeeding.

The text in your hands may be informative and helpful, but it can't give you that personal support you need when you begin breastfeeding. There are too many women who claim they were unable to breastfeed their baby. You don't want to be one of them. You may benefit from personal support.

For such support, I encourage you to attend breastfeeding meetings for support while you are pregnant. La Leche League meetings[4] are available in many communities and are a good source of support and information. Some churches and communities provide breastfeeding meetings; "café" meetings seem to be growing in popularity in some churches and communities. The Catholic Nursing Mothers League[5] provides spiritual support and encouragement for Catholic women in the hopes that mothers will nurse for at least a year. This League will be teaching the Seven Standards for breastfeeding duration as well as for natural spacing. It is important in a bottle-feeding society to find a group of successful breastfeeding mothers who want to offer other new mothers support. Try to find such a group in your community during your pregnancy.

There are many good books on breastfeeding, such as La Leche League's *The Womanly Art of Breastfeeding*. I recommend reading such a book during early pregnancy. Your birthing experience may influence your baby's suckling response. There are excellent books on childbirth, one being *The Birth Book* by Martha and Dr. William Sears. Due to the high c-section rate, about 30% today, you would do well to check on the c-section rate of doctors before choosing one for the birth of your baby. In some areas couples can choose the services of a midwife as an option.[6]

Some communities offer childbirth classes which teach the natural process of birthing and are very helpful. I encourage women to give birth in a vertical position, if at all possible; the gravity opens up the cervix more and the baby usually comes more quickly.

Some mothers offer professional support by working for other mothers as "doulas."[7] Doulas act as a childbirth advocate and helper at the time of childbirth. One of our daughters and her husband were so appreciative of their doula that they sent her a bouquet of roses after their childbirth experience. In addition, some doulas help breastfeeding mothers with household tasks and other children so the mother can care primarily for the baby.

What if I can't breastfeed?

This is like asking "What if I can't swim?" There will always be a few people who for various reasons are unable to learn how to swim. Likewise, there are the rare few mothers who are not successful at breastfeeding. I know a mother who made every possible effort to breastfeed her baby. As I learned what she went through, I had nothing but admiration and compassion for her. Mothers like her should never feel a moment of guilt. Regret is only natural, but they know they gave it their very best effort. While some mothers will have this unfortunate situation, they can still experience the joys of mothering and follow much of the counsel in this book. You can still be close and in touch with your child, hold him for bottle-feeding times, sleep with him, and enjoy and love him. Remember that you are that most important person to your baby. You, the mother, are more important than the milk. Here is the experience of one mother who was unable to breastfeed. She considered this a handicap.

> I was mothering our first baby the "natural mothering" way but with a bottle because I thought I was unable to nurse. I experienced the identical sleep cycles. We napped together, slept together, and woke together continuously for the first year, although she did sleep at night in a crib when she turned 11 months. I told myself that bottle-feeding was like a handicap that I had to overcome. I would think that if I were a wheelchair-bound mother, I wouldn't be able to run with my child, but I could still have a rich, loving relationship. So, I looked upon my inability to breastfeed as a handicap to overcome. I am now breastfeeding our second baby and it is everything I had imagined. It has been sheer bliss.

May you find the support you need when initiating breastfeeding and later may you in turn help others to have the good breastfeeding experience they desire. Gradually, breastfeeding may become the norm once again. Breastfeeding does space babies when the Seven Standards of Ecological Breastfeeding are followed.

> Everything has been going so well! I just had my first postpartum cycle following the birth of my almost 18-month-old son. Everything clicked right back on. After both children, I had no transition period. Just a few weeks of unmistakable mucus to get my attention, then right back to normal cycles. I was very pleased. After such a long time without charting (26 months), I was afraid a transitory time would really challenge my skills. I've only had 10 periods in 6½ years.

* * *

> The assurance I got from my husband was what I needed. He really acted as a buffer against the relatives and friends. My doctor was a tremendous help by his positive attitude. It also helped to be able to quote his remarks to the relatives.

* * *

I read your book *Breastfeeding and Natural Child Spacing* when I was pregnant and I found it very inspiring and helpful. I went 21 months without cycling after my first was born and 25 months after my second was born. My third son is 7 months old and I am not cycling yet. My husband and I do not really use the Billings method or the sympto-thermal method. I have found that breastfeeding is enough.

* * *

I'm new at NFP. I didn't practice ecological breastfeeding with my daughter and got pregnant with our son when our daughter was 6 months old. I'm still nursing my son who is 13 months old and JUST got my cycle back. I've been charting for a week now and I'm loving it. So many of my friends use medical ways to control their fertility. I feel it is so harmful to the body. I'm so thankful for groups like this and glad I googled NFP!

1. Frank-Hermann, P. et al. "The effectiveness of a fertility awareness based method to avoid pregnancy in relation to a couple's sexual behaviour during the fertile time: a prospective longitudinal study," *Human Reproduction*, February 20, 2007.
2. Ibid.
3. Shannon, Marilyn. *Fertility, Cycles and Nutrition*, Cincinnati: The Couple to Couple League, 2001. Available at www.nfpandmore.org.
4. La Leche League International: www.llli.org.
5. Catholic Nursing Mothers League: www.catholicbreastfeeding.org.
6. A list of midwives by area can be viewed at www.christianmidwives.org.
7. Information for doulas is at www.dona.org.

The Seven Standards Summary

Basic Principles

1. Frequent and unrestricted nursing is the primary factor in producing natural lactation amenorrhea and infertility. (Lactation amenorrhea is the absence of menstruation due to breastfeeding.)

2. Ecological breastfeeding (EBF) according to the Seven Standards below almost always provides this frequent nursing and natural infertility. It is that type of baby care which follows the natural mother-baby relationship. It avoids the use of artifacts and mother substitutes; it follows the baby-initiated patterns. EBF is the norm and offers many built-in benefits, one of which is extended natural infertility. A lengthy postpartum amenorrhea is the norm.

3. The following Seven Standards help to ensure this frequent nursing.

The Seven Standards: Phase 1 of Ecological Breastfeeding

This phase almost invariably produces natural infertility as long as the program is complete.

1. Breastfeed exclusively for the first six months of life; don't use other liquids and solids, not even water.
2. Pacify or comfort your baby at your breasts.
3. Don't use bottles and don't use pacifiers.
4. Sleep with your baby for night feedings.
5. Sleep with your baby for a daily-nap feeding.
6. Nurse frequently day and night, and avoid schedules.
7. Avoid any practice that restricts nursing or separates you from your baby.

Phase 1 is the time of exclusive breastfeeding and thus usually lasts six to eight months.

The Six Standards: Phase 2 of Ecological Breastfeeding

• Phase 2 of EBF begins when your baby starts taking solids or liquids other than breast milk.

• You begin to give liquids when your baby shows an interest in the cup, usually after six months.

• Aside from Standard #1, the other Six Standards of Phase 1 will remain operative until the baby gradually loses interest in breastfeeding. Phase 2 is a situation in which the **frequency** and **amount** of nursing is 1) not decreased at all at first, and 2) lessened only gradually at baby's pace. Phase 2 is frequently longer than Phase 1 with regard to natural infertility **if** EBF continues with frequent and unrestricted nursing.

Return of Fertility

The first 6 months. The *first 8 weeks postpartum* for the exclusively breastfeeding mother are so infertile that in 1988 scientists agreed that any vaginal bleeding during the first 56 days postpartum can be ignored for determining amenorrhea or fertility for the exclusively breastfeeding mother. This rule applies to the EBF mother.

During the *first 3 months postpartum*, the chance of pregnancy occurring is practically nil **if** the EBF mother remains in amenorrhea. Because of the above paragraph, this means the mother has no menstrual bleeding after the 56th postpartum day.

During the *next 3 months postpartum*, there is only a 1% chance of pregnancy **if** the EBF mother continues to remain in amenorrhea.

After 6 months. For the nursing mother there is only about a 6% chance of pregnancy occurring prior to the first menstruation. This assumes no fertility awareness and unrestricted intercourse. This risk can be reduced to close to 1% through the techniques of systematic natural family planning—observing the signs of fertility and abstaining accordingly.

Natural Spacing by Breastfeeding Alone

About 70% of EBF mothers experience their first menstruation between 9 and 20 months postpartum. The average return of menstruation for EBF mothers in the North American culture is between 14 and 15 months. For those couples who desire 18 to 30 months between the births of their children, ecological breastfeeding will usually be sufficient.

---

1. "The Seven Standards Summary" above is available on one page at nfpandmore.org. It can be searched at the top of the page or click on "NFP Resources" and then "Breastfeeding Infertility Research."

Breastfeeding Survey

I invite breastfeeding mothers to participate in an ongoing survey. You can obtain the survey form by going to **www.nfpandmore.org** and searching "breastfeeding survey" in the "Search" area at the top of the website.

The best way to complete this survey is in stages when they happen during a breastfeeding experience; that will take one or two years for some mothers. That's called a "prospective" survey. We are also happy to receive surveys completed shortly after the completion of the nursing experience when everything is fresh in your memory. That's called a "retrospective" survey. Both kinds are valuable for our continuing research.

You can photocopy this survey to share with others. I thank you for your help.

Made in the USA
Lexington, KY
02 April 2010